D0356821

THE PERILOUS SEARCH FOR THE PAST

In the early nineteen hundreds, a Greek sponge diver hunting at the bottom of the sea off the coast of Tunisia discovered some ancient marble columns. That was the beginning of underwater archaeology. Since then countless men have plunged into the sea, risking their lives to unlock the great secrets of the underwater world. These are their stories.

SUNKEN HISTORY

"Real excitement and suspense . . . Should lead many young people to consider a career in this fascinating field."
Best Sellers

"Endlessly fascinating . . . Absorbing."
Library Journal

BANTAM PATHFINDER EDITIONS

Bantam Pathfinder Editions provide the best in fiction and nonfiction in a wide variety of subject areas. They include novels by classic and contemporary writers; vivid, accurate histories and biographies; authoritative works in the sciences; collections of short stories, plays and poetry.

Bantam Pathfinder Editions are carefully selected and approved. They are durably bound, printed on specially selected high-quality paper, and presented in a new and handsome format.

SUNKEN HISTORY
The Story of Underwater Archaeology

BY ROBERT SILVERBERG

BANTAM BOOKS

BANTAM PATHFINDER EDITIONS
NEW YORK / TORONTO / LONDON

*This low-priced Bantam Book
has been completely reset in a type face
designed for easy reading, and was printed
from new plates. It contains the complete
text of the original hard-cover edition.*
NOT ONE WORD HAS BEEN OMTTED.

RLI: $\dfrac{\text{VLM } 8}{\text{IL } 7.12}$

SUNKEN HISTORY

*A Bantam Book / published by arrangement with
Chilton Books*

PRINTING HISTORY
*Chilton edition published April 1963
Literary Guild, Young Adults' Division, selection May 1963
Bantam Pathfinder edition published November 1964*

*Bantam Books are published by Bantam Books, Inc. Its trade-mark,
consisting of the words "Bantam Books" and the portrayal of a
bantam, is registered in the United States Patent Office and in other
countries. Marca Registrada. Printed in the United States of America. Bantam Books, Inc., 271 Madison Ave., New York 16, N. Y.*

This one is for HENRY

Introduction

To EXPLORE—to examine—above all, to understand. Men have been driven by these needs since they first walked the earth. Adventurous seamen, sailing beyond the ends of the known world to find out what was there; Galileo, risking imprisonment to turn an inquisitive eye toward the stars and planets; Vesalius, working secretly to uncover the mysteries of the human anatomy—all these men followed the same compulsion. Even with their lives at stake, they probed onward, for they had to *know*.

Today, man's curiosity has led him into a thousand endeavors. Space satellites whirl through the heavens, laying bare the secrets of the galaxy. Explorers roam the wilds of New Guinea and the frozen wastes of Antarctica. Atomic particles career and collide in cyclotrons as man exposes the essence of matter itself.

The war against ignorance continues on scores of battlefronts. One of the most exciting aspects of this endless campaign to know more about the world and man's place in it is the science of archaeology—the study of the remains of the past.

In an earlier book (*Lost Cities and Vanished Civilizations*, Chilton, 1962), I told of some of the earlier triumphs of archaeology: the recapture from time's grasp of cities like Pompeii, Babylon, Chichén Itzá, Knossos, Troy, and Angkor. From its beginning only two hundred years ago, at the volcano-buried city of Pompeii, archaeology has grown until it has become one of the most exciting, perhaps the most romantic, of all sciences. Entire nations long forgotten have yielded up their secrets, so that we now can reconstruct scenes of daily life in Egypt of three thousand years ago or Sumer of four thousand years ago with confidence.

Archaeology, as it was portrayed in *Lost Cities and Vanished Civilizations*, was shown largely as a matter of digging—of patient toil with pickax and knife under the sizzling tropic sun. And, indeed, for such archaeological pioneers as Layard and Schliemann, Evans and Koldewey, archaeology meant work on dry land.

But in our century, and particularly in the last twenty-five years, the archaeologists have extended their domain. The new field of underwater archaeology has come into being. Although the task of land archaeology is by no means complete, the underwater archaeologists are engaged in campaigns that promise to yield new secrets of yesterday. The pioneering work of land archaeology has already been done. Now, thanks to new techniques, archaeologists are turning to the sea. In Central America, in the Mediterranean, in dozens of sites throughout the world, exciting new finds are adding to our store of knowledge.

This is the story of this new development in man's quest for understanding: the story of underwater archaeology.

Contents

Chapter 1

Archaeology Turns to the Sea

T HE purpose of archaeology is to illustrate and to discover the course of human civilization." Those are the words of Sir Leonard Woolley, the great archaeologist who discovered Ur, the city of Abraham.

Some people seem to think the purpose of archaeology is to find beautiful objects of the past—statues and mosaics and temples. Certainly, the objects discovered by the archaeologists have added greatly to our artistic heritage. Who could fail to be fascinated by and to admire the beauty of such an archaeological find as the statuette of the ram in the thicket, discovered by Woolley at Ur and now at the University Museum in Philadelphia? Who does not take pleasure in the cool elegance of the murals found on Crete by Sir Arthur Evans in the palace of King Minos? And certainly, to see a shield which may have been used by Achilles, a mask that could have been worn by Agamemnon, is to enter into the world of the *Iliad* in a way that no mere reading of Homer can provide.

But these are only by-products of archaeology. To quote Leonard Woolley again, "The archaeologist, being after all human, does enjoy finding rare and beautiful objects, but wants to know all about them, and in any case prefers the acquisition of knowledge to that of things; for him digging consists very largely in observation, recording and interpretation."

It was not always this way. The early archaeologists were more interested in stocking museums with objects of art than they were in observing, recording, and interpreting. Tremendous damage was done by these men. They meant well, of course—but as they blundered into the buried cities, laying about them with pick and shovel, they destroyed irreplaceable evidence of the past in their feverish hunt for museum pieces.

Gradually, late in the nineteenth century, a new kind of archaeology developed. Instead of digging hastily into a site, the new archaeologists worked slowly, methodically. They would uncover a few feet at a time, stopping to record everything they saw—*everything*. Bits of pottery, crumbled brick, scattered rusty nails, even a fine chalky line where a wooden wall once had been—all this was written down and photographed in its original place before any attempt was made to dig deeper.

Later on, the archaeologist would publish his findings. Then everyone could conjecture about their meaning. Perhaps a bit of broken pottery found in Mesopotamia could be matched in workmanship and design with a similar fragment found in India. Then an important fact about the past would have been revealed: that there was commerce between Mesopotamia and India in the remote past. Bits of pottery do not look very attractive in a museum display case, but they have been tremendously important in helping the archaeologist understand and reveal the meaning of man's past.

So, archaeology today is not just a matter of digging up buried treasure. The archaeologist seeks to learn how men built their homes, what foods they ate, what weapons they used, how they dressed, how they worshipped their gods. And to discover these things means careful, methodical, inch-by-inch excavation. The archaeologist feels a great responsibility to do his job perfectly. If, through ignorance or carelessness, he destroys part of the evidence, he is hindering rather than aiding the advance of human knowledge.

The archaeologist who works in the sea is subject to the same rules. He, too, must be methodical and precise. He, too, must photograph and record every minute detail before he disturbs it. But his job is fantastically difficult. Instead of contending with the hot sun, he must carry out his work under the weight of tons of water. He is menaced by sharks, barracuda, and other predators of the depths. He often must work at a site that is buried not simply by sand or vegetation, but by barnacles, clams, coral growths, or solid limestone. And while he works, his very life rests on the source of oxygen that keeps him breathing.

Despite these handicaps, the underwater archaeologist has no hesitations about tackling his assignments—and, indeed, he welcomes the dangers of his profession. Working in the sea provides an extra dimension to archaeology. The "professors with fins" work with the awareness that they are on the frontier of man's domain. Like spacemen, they venture beyond the realm of the atmosphere in the name of science.

There are four general types of sites where the underwater archaeologist works. In the chapters to come, we'll have a close look at each, but let's see just now what they are.

ANCIENT SHIPWRECKS

So far, this category has proven to be one of the most fertile for the underwater archaeologist. Shipping has always been a risky endeavor. Each year some ships are lost. In the days of the Greeks and Romans, the Mediterranean was dotted with trading vessels, and tragedy struck frequently and without warning. A darkening of the sky, a sudden storm, and a majestic ship bound for Spain or North Africa might capsize in a moment. To the bottom it would go, bearing all hands down—and taking with it its cargo. The Mediterranean is littered with the remains of ships of all ages, going back to the dawn of shipping some four or five thousand years ago.

It has never been any secret that these ships were down there. The problem was to reach them, to bring up the treasure trapped in their rotting holds. Although, as we will see, fishermen now and then brought up some fragment of a statue, some slime-encrusted vase, such finds were rare and only served to remind archaeologists of the wonders beyond reach.

As recently as 1928, the classical scholar Salomon Reinach wrote, "The richest museum of antiquities in the world is still inaccessible to us. It lies at the bottom of the eastern Mediterranean. We are able to explore the land and the air without much difficulty, but we are very far from rivalling the fish in their element, who, in the words of Saint Augustine, have their being in the secret ways of the abyss. Those ways remain closed to us.

"Whilst awaiting the day when the progress of science will permit us to engage in that exploration, the archaeologist already owes some magnificent underwater discoveries to chance and the fisherman."

Today the secret ways of the abyss are no longer closed to us. Archaeologists are eagerly roaming the depths of the Mediterranean, and its sunken museum is yielding up its treasures one by one.

SUBMERGED SHORE AREAS

Another important phase of underwater archaeology is the exploration of regions that once were on dry land but which now are invaded by the sea. Over thousands of years, shore lines change. In some parts of the world, the sea retreats, revealing what had once been the ocean bottom. In other places, the sea encroaches on the land, nibbling away foot by foot.

Some of the best sites for underwater archaeology have resulted from this nibbling-away process. Most of them are along the shores of the Mediterranean, which, so far, is the center of most of the underwater archaeological activity. The ancient Roman port of Caesarea, in what is now Israel, is one such site. The encroaching sea has drowned part of the harbor; the archaeologists are now at work recapturing it from the Mediterranean. Elsewhere around the fringes of that sea, the ruins of ancient cities can be seen just off the shore, and each in turn will receive the attentions of the archaeologist.

SUNKEN CITIES

Sometimes not just a shore line, but an entire city is drowned by a sudden cataclysm. Some archaeologists believe that the Biblical cities of Sodom and Gomorrah perished this way, the land giving way and sinking so that the waters of the Dead Sea poured over them. Then, too, there is the semi-mythical city of Ys off the coast of Brittany, and even fabled Atlantis, the legendary sunken continent that men have dreamed of finding since Plato's time. Recently the earthquake-drowned city of Port Royal, on the island of Jamaica, has been explored by archaeologists. In a later chapter there will be more about the quests for Atlantis, for Ys, and the other sunken cities of the world.

SACRIFICIAL WELLS

The fourth major category of underwater archaeology is the well used for sacrifices. Throwing objects into a well seems to be almost universally considered a way of guaranteeing good luck. Who has not tossed a coin into a wishing well at some time?

There have been nations who believed in throwing more

than small change into wells for good luck. Most particularly, the Mayas of Central America, who held regular ceremonies in which human beings were sacrificed to the gods by being hurled into deep wells. Along with the helpless victims, the Mayas would hurl jewelry and other gifts for the gods.

In *Lost Cities and Vanished Civilizations* I told how E. H. Thompson explored the sacrificial well at Chichén Itzá in Mexico. Thompson, one of the pioneers of underwater archaeology, used clumsy dredges and crude, awkward diving suits to enter the depths of the muddy well. His yield was great; articles of copper, gold, and jade by the hundred emerged from the well.

A few years ago, a modern expedition descended into the well at Chichén Itzá to see if Thompson had left anything behind. Elsewhere in the land of the Mayas, other searchers are exploring wells and lakes where these strange Indians left myriad relics of their civilization.

In order to plumb the depths of the sea, man has had to deal with two big problems: the problem of breathing, and the problem of pressure.

The earliest divers simply held their breath. In many parts of the world today, pearl divers and fish hunters still make use of that most elementary of diving techniques. But the amount of exploration that can be done on each dive is limited. The most skilled of divers can hold his breath only two or three minutes at the extreme. The ordinary untrained swimmer usually runs out of breath in less than a minute. No archaeologist could possibly carry out any kind of investigation in one-minute bursts. So before there could be any science of underwater archaeology, there had to be some way of carrying a breathing supply into the depths.

Pressure complicates the situation. At a depth of thirty-three feet, the water presses in on every square inch of a diver's body with twice the force of the air at the surface. When he goes down to sixty-six feet, the pressure is triple that at the surface, at ninety-nine feet quadruple, and so on. As the diver descends, it is as though an invisible fist is squeezing him—tighter, tighter, always tighter. The eyeballs are pushed inward. The eardrums are pushed inward. The lungs are compressed. It is not a pleasant sensation.

An unprotected diver can go down as deep as two hundred feet without suffering too seriously from pressure. Beyond that point, though, some kind of armor is needed. Men have descended thousands of feet within the bathyscaphe, whose thick metal walls resist the pressure. If the bathyscaphe's walls ever yielded, the men inside would be crushed flat by the pressure of the water.

Most underwater archaeology is carried on at depths where the pressure is not an overwhelming drawback. But the problem of breathing is something else again.

The story of underwater diving is a long one, and would need a book of its own. Diving bells and diving suits go back to the Middle Ages. From the nineteenth century on, improvements came rapidly, so that the modern diving suit enables a diver to walk around in safety and even comfort at great depths. His air supply reaches him through a pipe from the surface far above.

Even a diving suit, though, is clumsy for shallow-water work. The diver must clank around inside a massive metallic shell that makes every movement cumbersome and ponderous. He is not free to roam as he pleases. And if his lifeline to the surface is cut, he is in serious trouble. A man in a diving suit is too vulnerable to accident and too hampered by the bulkiness of his equipment.

Diving suits are necessary for work at great depths, where the body would otherwise be crushed by water pressure. But since the bulk of underwater archaeology sites are no more than one or two hundred feet below the surface, something simpler, more convenient was called for.

We have it today. It is known as "SCUBA"—short for Self-Contained Underwater Breathing Apparatus. SCUBA has created a revolution in undersea archaeology. It liberates divers from the risky dependency on an air hose, and it frees them from the confines of the diving suit. Clad only in mask, swimsuit, and flippers, the SCUBA-diver carries his breathing supply with him, and moves about as he pleases. Today nearly all underwater archaeology is carried on by SCUBA-divers, or skin divers, except where depth is a problem.

The SCUBA revolution is quite new, though the idea of self-contained diving apparatus goes back almost 150 years. The first one was invented by W. H. James in 1825. It made use of an oxygen cylinder coupled to a conventional diving suit of that era.

But when we breathe, we give off carbon dioxide, which in large quantities becomes poisonous. The W. H. James apparatus allowed carbon dioxide (CO_2) to collect in the breathing supply. Soon the oxygen supply was fouled by CO_2, and the diver had to return to the surface.

Not until 1878 did anyone perfect a self-contained apparatus that effectively got rid of the exhaled CO_2. The invention of H. A. Fleuss of England circulated oxygen continuously. The CO_2 was chemically removed and disposed of through a valve. But this device, though it was useful in its way, was not adapted for swimmers. It could only be used by someone walking with weighted feet on the ocean bottom.

Skin diving, as we know it today, got started about 1933, in France. Commandant Yves le Prieur, a French naval officer, invented a SCUBA rig that consisted of a bottle of compressed air slung on the chest, linked by an airpipe to a face mask covering the entire face. Even with this, swimming was not possible. The diver had to walk on the bottom. But in the next decade engineers all over the world worked to modify the original device. At the same time, flippers to aid in swimming were developed, a Frenchman named de Corlieu putting the first rubber foot-fins on the market in 1935. (Leonardo da Vinci has thought of the idea of using hand-flippers four hundred years earlier, and Benjamin Franklin had actually made a pair.)

World War II saw the development of underwater breathing equipment for military uses. The U.S. Navy's "frogmen" had oxygen equipment that allowed them to spend two hours at a time under water without surfacing. But this apparatus was good only to a depth of thirty-three feet. Below that, the diver was likely to get oxygen poisoning as a result of breathing pure oxygen.

After the war, surplus "rebreathers" from war stock were sold to the public, and skin diving became a popular fad among the adventurous. But these early rebreathers were dangerous and caused many deaths when divers went too deep. At depths of more than thirty-three feet, or two atmospheres, the blood absorbs oxygen too easily, and quickly becomes saturated with it. The result is that the oxygen-saturated blood is unable to carry away carbon dioxide properly, and death follows swiftly.

When it became known how dangerous rebreathing devices were, the inventors got busy again. Attention turned to "open-circuit" breathing apparatus.

The dangerous oxygen rebreathers were termed "closed-circuit" devices because the same supply of oxygen cir-

culated endlessly, with CO_2 and other impurities being
drawn off. "Open-circuit" units—in which exhaled air is dis-
carded into the water—were considered to be much safer
for various technical reasons.

But open-circuit systems had one big flaw. They ran out
of air too soon. With a closed-circuit system, a diver could
stay under water for hours. The open-circuit system fed air
constantly, and the supply was soon used up, making it necessary to return to the surface within just a few minutes, or
else to carry crushingly heavy tanks.

What was needed was some sort of valve that would slow
down the consumption of air in the open-circuit system.
Strangely, the basic idea for this valve had been patented
all the way back in 1866. A Parisian inventor named
Benoist Rouquarol had perfected the apparatus now called
a "demand regulator." Demand regulators adjust themselves
to the pressure of the water surrounding the diver, and give
air only when the diver inhales. With a demand regulator
controlling the output of air from the tanks, open-circuit
apparatus could carry half an hour or more of air.

Rouquarol, in 1866, was ahead of his time, and his invention never caught on. But, ninety years later, the world
was ready for it. Demand regulators were adapted to create
safe, efficient open-circuit SCUBA.

A lean, hawk-faced Frenchman named Jacques-Yves
Cousteau, whom we will meet again and again in the
chapters to come, had the first success with this kind of
equipment. He and an engineer named Emile Gagnan developed their apparatus in 1943, and made over 500 dives
with it that year, going down to the depths of 60 and 70
feet, then, cautiously, to 130 feet, and then to the amazing
depth of 210 feet.

Cousteau and Gagnan received a United States Patent
for their equipment in March, 1947. It was called the "Aqua
Lung." This is a trade name that refers only to the Cou-
steau-Gagnan apparatus. But, like such other trade names as
victrola and frigidaire, aqualung has become part of our
language. We use it today to refer to any kind of SCUBA
device, not just the one patented by Cousteau and Gagnan.

Many different types of aqualungs are on the market nowadays, more than a decade and a half after the first ones
were sold to the public. Yet the basic principle is pretty
much the same in all of them. The diver carries tanks of
compressed air—not pure oxygen—on his back. A hose carries the air to the diver's mouthpiece, and the demand regu-

lator provides him with air as he needs it. Stale air goes out through an exhaust valve. The diver wears a mask and flippers, and where the water is cold he may wear a rubberized suit that covers his entire body.

Using SCUBA equipment today is almost as simple as swimming itself, and many youngsters from the age of ten up have tried their skills at it—with proper supervision, of course. It takes a few lessons in a swimming pool or in very shallow water to master the fundamentals and to learn what to do in case of an emergency. The novice has to know exactly what to do in case his air hose is punctured or if his masks fills with water.

But these basics can be acquired in a couple of hours of training. And then the undersea world—the world that Captain Cousteau has called, in a famous book, *The Silent World*—lies before you, waiting to be conquered.

Skin diving is the closest thing to actual free flight that any of us will ever experience. You slide beneath the surface, and weight vanishes. You are not aware of the tanks on your back. If you go down, as I did, in the crystal-clear waters of the Caribbean, you quickly lose all sense of being in water at all. The waves are above you. The water is utterly transparent. You look down and see the branching beauty of a staghorn coral formation. A kick of your flippers and you are gliding down, fifteen, twenty, twenty-five feet. You inspect the coral at close range, while fearless little fish of rainbow hues inspect *you*, sometimes actually bumping into your face mask in their curiosity. Perhaps an armada of foot-long squid, swimming in tight military formation, will pass above you. You kick your flippers again, and soar effortlessly upward for a better look. The squid, without losing their dignity, squirt brown fluid into the water and swim away from you.

It is a timeless world, and the pity of it is that you must return to the surface when your tanks approach exhaustion. It is often a struggle to force yourself to leave. Under the water, you are utterly free, free to move about as you please, upward, downward, in any direction. Only when you return to dry land do you become the slave of gravity once again.

Most of the amateur skin divers never go down deeper than thirty feet or so. But—if proper precautions are taken—a skilled diver can go to depths nearly ten times as great. There are dangers, of course—but there are also tremendous rewards.

The coming of SCUBA transformed underwater archaeology. Gone were the clumsy diving suits, gone the weighted shoes that kicked up clouds of sediment and disturbed the relics of the ages. Now the archaeologist could move about at will, examining, photographing, studying. When delicate work had to be done, he could do it with his own hands, not even needing gloves.

Of course, not all archaeologists are able to skin dive. Even so, they can make use of the athletic skills of others. Archaeologists who are not themselves agile or youthful enough to don an aqualung can and do direct the activities of others. Expeditions have been headed successfully by men who never get into a bathing suit.

Every archaeologist, though, prefers to see with his own eyes. And so a new breed of younger archaeologists is evolving—the archaeologist-skin diver—who is not only able to make dives, but who is trained in the science of interpreting what he sees.

So popular has underwater archaeology become, in fact, that some professional archaeologists are becoming concerned about its public appeal. Thus, in a conference on underwater archaeology held by the Minnesota Historical Society in 1963, the director of New York's Adirondack Museum said he was "sick to death of skin divers" who disturb sunken archaeological treasures. The official, Robert B. Inverarity, declared, "It's like fighting off the enemy, and we are also fighting off amateur historians and archaeologists who think they are experts." So underwater archaeology has now come to share one of the biggest problems of its land counterpart—the amateur antiquity-hunter.

Since safe and satisfactory SCUBA equipment has been widely available only since 1947, underwater archaeology is still in its first flush of activity. SCUBA—and other new gadgets such as the Link Air Lift, which we will meet in later chapters—opens an entire new world for the archaeologist.

Before we start to examine the progress that the young science of underwater archaeology has made, though, let's go back to the days before the aqualung—to the pioneering days of underwater archaeology.

Chapter 2

Fishermen and Sponge Divers

THE year was 1900. A storm raged on the Mediterranean—a howling northwestern wind. It spelled danger for any ships unlucky enough to be caught out at sea. For thousands of years, just such storms had been sending Greek vessels to the bottom.

And now two Greek ships were in danger, sailing galleys carrying sponge divers. Century after century, rugged, muscular Greeks had plunged to the bottom of the Mediterranean to rip sponges free. Without benefit of helmets or air tanks, they hurtled downward, weighting their feet with stones, and harvested sponges until their mighty lungs were drained of air. Then, kicking free of their weights, they would rise to the surface with their booty.

The two ships were on their way home from North Africa, where the divers had been gathering sponges off the coast of Tunisia. When the sudden storm blew up, the galleys were forced to take refuge. They pulled in off the island of Antikythera, at the very tip of the Greek archipelago, not far from Crete. They dropped anchor in a quiet cove, the ships resting some seventy-five feet offshore.

It looked as though they would be stranded there for some while until the storm blew itself out. The Captain, Demetrios Kondos, had a thrifty idea. "As long as we have to stay here anyway, why not see if there are sponges to be harvested?"

These Greeks, descendants of the ancient *sphoungarades*, or sponge divers, used modern methods—helmets, weighted boots. Diver Elias Stadiatis suited up, clambered over the side. Down through 150 feet of clear water he dove, to the bottom.

Sponges were forgotten in sudden excitement. What was

this? Horses at the bottom of the sea? Giant men and women? Was this some abode of the gods?

No. Not gods. Statues.

Dazed, Stadiatis peered at the confused tangle of statuary. There, half-buried in sand, stood a goddess of marble, naked and beautiful to behold from the back, her face eaten away by shellfish. And there, huge horses, their hooves raking at the water as though they were about to gallop to the surface. There, the blind eyes of a muscular young man stared intently at a passing fish.

Stadiatis reached toward the hand of a nearby bronze statue, clasped it. An entire arm came off in his grip. Clutching the massive arm tightly, he yanked wildly on his line.

"Pull me up! Pull me up!"

He came to the surface, displayed his find. Pointing toward the sea, he gasped out, "Statues—horses, men, gods, dozens of statues!"

But the storm was lifting. Besides, the two galleys were not equipped for bringing up heavy statues from the depths. Carefully, Captain Kondos noted down the exact location of the site, after going down himself to verify the find and take measurements of the statues. Then the two galleys set sail for home.

Captain Kondos and the diver Stadiatis journeyed to Athens with their story, and the giant arm as evidence. The sponge gatherers were welcomed joyously. For centuries, other countries had been plundering the antiquities of Greece, but now Greece had some archaeologists of her own, and they relished the chance to find hitherto unknown treasures. An expedition was quickly organized. By November, 1900, a vessel of the Greek Navy, equipped for handling the big statues, was moored at the Antikythera site.

The archaeologists and divers worked for nine months. For most of the time, strong winds were blowing, endangering the ships. The divers had a hard time of it too. They had to work at depths of 150 to 170 feet, and their crude diving equipment offered them little protection against the pressure. They could stay down no more than five or six minutes at a time, and, as it was, two of them were disabled by the bends, a disease that cripples divers who come up too fast from great depths. One of the divers died.

Despite all these handicaps, the results were impressive.

The men were able to pull loose a life-sized bronze head, two large marble statues, and a few smaller pieces. Other expeditions in the next few years found dozens of additional statues at the site. Bringing the finds to the surface posed problems. They had to be maneuvered into sturdy slings—and, if a statue slipped from its sling, it would destroy itself and anything it landed on.

The statues were taken to Athens, where they were examined by a Greek archaeologist, Professor George Karo. Although one might think that the divers would have damaged the statues in lifting them, Professor Karo wrote, "These illiterate fishermen, totally ignorant of archaeological techniques, treated the finds with quite remarkable care and delicacy. I was amazed at the insignificant amount of recent damage. Not only had the sculptures been handled with evident gentleness, but even pottery and glass vases had been brought up intact."

The Antikythera Expedition of 1900–1901 is an important milestone in the history of archaeology. It was the first time that any serious attempt had been made to recover antiquities from the sea.

There had been earlier finds, but on a random, scatter-shot basis. Pausanias, who wrote in the second century after Christ, remarked that the "fishermen of Methymna, having cast their nets into the sea, drew them in and discovered a head carved from the wood of the olive tree." For many centuries afterward, fishermen had been making such unexpected finds as they hauled in their nets.

But it was a hit-or-miss business that had nothing to do with systematic archaeology. In 1877 a bronze figurehead of the Gorgon Medusa came to light off the coast of France, but it was sold for scrap metal. A bronze statue of Apollo, hauled in near the island of Elba some years earlier, fared better and is now in the Louvre. Most of the museums of Europe displayed one or more pieces of sculpture that had thus been retrieved from the sea.

But at Antikythera an entire group of antiquities was rescued at the same time. This provided some insight into the past that single statues, or fragments, could not offer.

The statues had gone to the bottom in a shipwreck, of course. They had been en route from Athens to Rome some time in the first century B.C. The date can be fixed quite exactly, for reasons which we shall see in a moment. The wrecked ship had been carrying both bronze statues and marble ones. The bronze statues were about four hundred years old at the time they went to the bottom—that is, they had been made during the time of Socrates and Plato. And they were superb in design. One authority, writing about the bronze statue now called *The Ephebe*, or *The Athlete*, says: "Classic art has no more beautiful gem in its rich store than this."

But the marbles were much younger. They had been only a few decades old at the time they were loaded aboard the ill-fated ship. They seemed to be latter-day copies of much older Greek statues. The marble statues had suffered badly from the effects of spending two thousand years in the sea. One expert who saw them wrote, "Imagine bodies licked by fire, debris covered with molluscs, men eaten away by some horrible malady. The marbles are very greatly corroded and none of the modelling is left. You can just divine beautiful shapes and attitudes."

An interesting point is that the leaden bases of the bronze statues were bent and torn, as though the statues had been ripped up violently. It is thought that the statues represent the booty of Roman marauders who looted the temples of Greece. Stealing hastily, they not only took valuable bronzes of great quality, but much newer and less important marble pieces. Perhaps they were part of the Roman raiding force that pillaged Greece in 86 B.C. under the dictator Sulla.

The most important single find of the Antikythera Expedition was not a statue at all—but a badly corroded lump of bronze that was hardly noticed at first. Statues by the thousands have survived the downfall of Greece and Rome, but this object is unique. It is nothing less than a highly complicated machine for performing mathematical computations!

At first it went unnoticed. It was tossed aside by the archaeologists who first examined the Antikythera finds, since it was so badly decayed as to be thought worthless. But, in 1902, the archaeologist Valerios Stais of the National Museum in Athens was sorting through a group of bronze fragments from Antikythera when he happened to notice something strange about this particular one.

He stared at it in amazement. "It seems to be some kind of mechanism!" Stais exclaimed.

A mechanism it was indeed. Many archaeologists studied the surprising find in detail, and it could plainly be seen that the object had dials, gear wheels, and inscribed plates. It was—and still is—the only mechanical object that has been preserved from ancient Greece. Although we knew that the Greeks were outstanding in scientific theory, we had not realized that they had cultivated the practical side of technology as well. Yet here was this device, with more than twenty gears intermeshed in a highly complicated way, to tell us that the Greeks had known more about machine-making than we had suspected.

The mechanism's inscribed plates also helped archaeologists to assign a definite date to the shipwreck. The lettering was in a style that was known to be no older than 100 B.C. and to have gone out of use around the time of Christ. And the words used in the inscription supported this observation. They included some astronomical data similar to that compiled by a Greek named Geminos about 77 B.C. The mechanism provided a clear and indisputable way of dating the wreck.

Discovering exactly what the mechanism's purpose had been took many years. First, the rust and calcification had to be cleared away. The dials and inscriptions left no doubt that it was some sort of astronomical device. For a long time archaeologists thought that it was a navigating instrument, perhaps an astrolabe (an instrument used for fixing a ship's position by the stars).

More than fifty years after the divers had brought the mysterious mechanism up, the job of cleaning it was finished. A London-born scholar, Derek J. De Solla Price, and a specialist in ancient Greek inscriptions, George Stamires, examined the mechanism in 1955. Their first success was to fit the various fragments of it together properly. Although it had been thought that the mechanism was distorted and squashed, Price and Stamires found that it was actually quite well preserved. Originally it had consisted of a wooden box with hinged doors, containing the gear mechanisms. It must have looked very much like an old clock. But the wooden parts had vanished over the twenty centuries of submersion.

Price and Stamires studied the intricate system of gears and dials and were impressed with the complexity of the device. One of the dials bore the signs of the zodiac, another the names of the months. As the gears turned, the instrument would provide information about the risings and settings of the important stars and constellations throughout the year. Other dials gave much more complicated astronomical information.

The two scholars reconstructed the device from its remnant and concluded that it had been used to calculate the positions of the heavenly bodies throughout the year. We had known that the Greeks had been excellent astronomers. But we had not been aware that they could translate their concepts into instrumentation of this sort. As Dr. Price wrote:

"The Antikythera mechanism was no flash in the pan but was part of an important current in Hellenistic civilization. History has contrived to keep that current dark to us, and only the accidental underwater preservation of fragments that would otherwise have crumbled to dust has now brought it to light. It is a bit frightening to know that just before the fall of their great civilization the ancient Greeks had come so close to our age, not only in their thought, but in their scientific technology."

The next important find in the Mediterranean came six years after the Antikythera discoveries. In June, 1907, Greek sponge divers were at work off Mahdia, a small port on the coast of Tunisia. Mahdia, an unimportant but ancient town, goes back to the days of the Phoenicians. Though nothing more than a fishing village today, it had been a harbor used by the vanished merchant marine fleets of Carthage, Greece, and Rome, hundreds of years before Christ. Caesar had stopped off there on a visit after his sojourn in Egypt with Cleopatra. In the Middle Ages it had been a pirate lair.

The sea is shallow at Mahdia, no more than about twenty fathoms deep, even three or four miles off shore. On the bottom, a thin layer of mud covers a rock shelf.

One day in June, 1907, a Greek sponge diver was prowling over that rock shelf, three miles off shore and 130 feet down, when he came across what looked like "a lot of big guns" on the sea bottom. A closer look told him that he saw not cannons but marble columns covered with mud. Scattered nearby were statues large and small, of both bronze and marble.

The diver hastily surfaced. Calling his comrades together, he pointed excitedly toward the water. "I have found treasure down there! Ancient treasure!"

The divers immediately abandoned their quest for sponges in favor of the more profitable harvest of antiquities. They brought up whatever was small enough to lift by hand. Taking their booty ashore, they sold it to antique dealers.

This has long been the plague of archaeology. Workmen or fishermen discover important antiquities and carry them away to be sold, usually for next to nothing. The finder does not profit greatly, and archaeology loses. For, once an object is moved from its surroundings, much valuable information is destroyed. The object is still important as a work of art, but its historical value is lost.

A few weeks after the sponge divers had sold their finds, a French archaeologist named Alfred Merlin was strolling through a native Tunisian *souk,* or bazaar. He was startled to find ancient and genuine Greek bowls, candelabras, and stone carvings for sale at ridiculously low prices.

Merlin bought the lot. Then he asked the dealers, "Where did these things come from?"

They answered him with a shrug. In that part of the world, no one gives information to a European willingly. But some money changed hands, and the tongues of the dealers were loosened.

"We bought them from Greek divers," Merlin was told. "They find these things in the sea and bring them to us."

Merlin immediately set out to protect what was left of the find and to see to it that it was explored scientifically. The Greek divers were politely informed that the antiquities were the property of the government of Tunisia, and that there would be no more private plunder. Then, to cover the enormous expense of an expedition—underwater archaeology is a far more costly proposition than landside excavation—Merlin raised money from a group of American and Parisian millionaires, got contributions from the Tunisian government as well as that of France, and set to work.

The Mahdia exploration still stands as one of the major archaeological accomplishments of the century. Under Merlin's supervision, six separate expeditions were organized between 1908 and 1911. The French Navy contributed the use of a tugboat, and the Board of Harbors supplied a diving boat. Even with this help, the Mahdia work was financially burdensome. Archaeologists on the land can usually work every day; underwater archaeologists are hampered by wind and storm, and sometimes find they can get no more than an hour or two of work accomplished a day, two or three days a week. And, all this while, ships and divers must stand idly by. Whereas on land most of the digging is done by low-paid native workers, underwater archaeology must be handled by skilled divers whose pay compensates them for the risks they take.

Merlin had all the usual problems of underwater archaeology. His divers—all Greek but for one lone Turk—demanded and received high wages. Sudden storms frequently carried away marker buoys, making it necessary for Merlin to find his sites over and over again. High winds hampered the work.

But the difficulties were worth enduring. On the bottom of the sea lay six rows of columns, sixty in number, covering a space about a hundred feet long. And, wrote Merlin, "All around lay a mass of marble fragments piled up in no sort of order—capitals and bases, carefully squared blocks, architectural elements of many different types. Mixed with these objects, and especially toward the northern end of the site, was a profusion of broken earthenware, all that remained of the pottery which had been on board—amphorae, very few of which were intact, vases of many kinds used for the carrying of oil, wine, water, foodstuffs, and ingredients needed by the crew during the voyage. . . . Further columns, marble blocks, amphorae, and anchors were found under a deep layer of mud from which they stuck out in a confused mass. Before any results could be achieved, it was necessary to move the various obstructions, and to dig into and clear away the enveloping slime."

The marble columns—a dozen feet long, two feet in diameter—interfered with the work of removing the smaller objects. Whenever a diver tried to slip a hawser under a column to lift it out of the way, he would kick up a cloud of mud that would surround him with an opaque darkness. The current, at the bottom, was so strong that the exhausted divers had to be brought to the surface after just a short period of work. But, Merlin wrote:

"When the men managed to dig under such of the columns as could be separated—or to work their way between them—they very soon came on a layer of timber, about eight inches thick, and in a condition, more or less, of decomposition. Penetration of this protective envelope brought to light objects of a more delicate type: bronze statuettes of fine workmanship, fragments of beautifully ornamented furniture.

"It seems clear that when the vessel foundered, she plunged straight to the bottom without breaking up, having sustained a certain amount of damage, but not turning turtle. The rotting timber had once been the ship's deck. The columns and some of the less fragile objects had rested upon it, the columns having been laid sufficiently far apart to make movement between them possible, and so as not to interfere with the handling of the vessel. The bales containing the smaller and more precious portions of the cargo were stowed between decks. The hold was filled with works of art in metal or marble."

Merlin also had some ideas on the fate of the ship. A storm, he thought, had driven it across the Mediterranean to the African coast line. Thick mist had shrouded the ship, lifting suddenly to reveal Africa not far off. The seamen, afraid of running aground, had tried to turn the ship and put out to sea again, but as they put it about, it may have heeled over and begun to fill with water. To steady the ship while they bailed it, the anchors were dropped. But the hull continued to fill with water, and soon the foundered ship had slipped below the surface, coming to rest with its precious cargo on the bottom.

The mud that made recovery such a chore had also served to preserve the statues. Whereas at Antikythera shellfish had bored into the marble, the Mahdia statues were clean and unmutilated. The mud yielded statue after statue, dozens in all, many of them of remarkable beauty. Today they fill six rooms at the Bardo Museum in Tunis. "Nothing comparable has come to light," the Hellenist Salomon Reinach wrote, "since Pompeii and Herculaneum."

The treasures of the Mahdia wreck are masterpieces of Greek art, and the world is all the richer to have them on display once again. However, lovely as the statues are, they formed only part of the treasure-trove of the foundered ship, and in the eyes of many archaeologists the statues are the least important part. Just as the masterpiece of the Antikythera ship was the astronomical computer, so, too, the most exciting finds at Mahdia are the least obvious ones.

Bronzes and marbles are delightful to look at. But they tell us little about the daily way of life in the ancient world. To find, as was done at Mahdia, cooking pots and lamps, gives us those small details about everyday living that make the past so much more vivid.

This is why Pompeii, for instance, is such an important archaeological treasure. When Mount Vesuvius erupted, Pompeii, Herculaneum, and other cities around the volcano were buried almost instantly by ash and lava. Thus, those cities remained just as they were on the day of their death, and archaeologists gained invaluable insight into ordinary ancient-world existence by excavating them.

A ship which sinks with all cargo intact is equally valuable, on a smaller scale. And so the small details of the

Mahdia wreck have helped us learn a bit more about the vanished past. The lamp with its charred wick still in place, the cooking utensils, the anchors and the ballast—these all illuminate the ancient world for us.

Archaeologists have established an amazing amount of information about the ship itself, not only why it sank, but where it came from, where it was probably heading, and when. By comparing the style of pottery found aboard with pottery whose dates were already known, the experts were able to decide that the Mahdia ship had gone down during the first century before Christ—about the same time as the Antikythera ship, perhaps even in the same storm. Inscribed Greek slabs found in the cargo indicate that the ship almost certainly sailed from Athens. And its cargo of bronze statuary and marbles, like that of the Antikythera ship, may have been booty plundered from the temples of Athens by the Roman soldiers who, under Sulla, invaded Greece in 86 B.C.

The Mahdia ship was badly overloaded. It contained a hodgepodge of works of art and unfinished marble blocks and columns, as though the plunderers had grabbed everything they could find, planning to sort out the useful from the useless in Rome. But the ship never reached Rome. Storm winds drove it far off course, to the African coast.

One part of the hypothesis bolsters another. If the ship was manned by Sulla's men, then its course was to Rome, and not to Africa, because at that time Africa was in the sway of Sulla's enemy, Marius. Maybe that was why the sailors swung the ship around so hurriedly when they realized they were near the African coast—and, as it turned, the overloaded ship foundered.

Merlin's work at Mahdia ended in 1913. The coming of the First World War put a general halt to archaeological work. After the war, the Mahdia site was not thought desirable for another full-scale archaeological expedition. Many private, smaller scale groups descended to explore the wreck, though. Even the Greeks returned to dive once more for sponges. Merlin's many expeditions had removed all the visible and portable antiquities, but this did not stop amateur archaeologists from having a go at the site.

In 1948, another serious expedition returned to the site. But in the forty years that had passed since Merlin's first expedition, the techniques of underwater exploration had changed tremendously. The aqualung had been invented, and it was now possible for freely swimming divers to inspect the wreck.

And so, Mahdia served as a training ground for the new breed of underwater archaeologists. A group of French skin divers—Jacques-Yves Cousteau, Philippe Tailliez, and Frederic Dumas—had banded together after World War II to form the Groupe de Recherches Sous-Marines, or Undersea Research Group. They had done salvage work in a number of Atlantic and Mediterranean harbors, using SCUBA equipment to find the wrecks of ships sunk during the war. Gradually they had become interested in archaeology, and excitement filled them when they learned of the vast number of Greek and Roman ships on the bottom of the Mediterranean.

In 1948, Cousteau and his friends were diving in North Africa, exploring the water off shore at the site of the ancient city of Carthage. Though that expedition came to naught, they visited the museum at Tunis and learned of Merlin's work decades earlier.

"Perhaps there is still some treasure left in the wreck," they told each other. "It's worth a try."

They read through the reports of Merlin's 1908–13 work, and contacted Merlin himself, elderly but still interested in archaeology, to tell him that they were going to return to his site at Mahdia. The old man gave the skin divers his enthusiastic blessing.

Finding the site, though, was no easy matter. Lieutenant Tavera, the French naval officer who had supervised Merlin's divers, had written a report giving the location of the site. Tavera had mentioned three landmarks—a castle, a small bush, and a windmill. Cousteau and his comrades found the ruined castle easily enough. But, as Cousteau tells it, "In the 35 years since Tavera had drawn the lonely bush, a veritable forest had grown up around it. The last clue was a change in color of a distant olive grove lined up on a foreground windmill. We squinted through the glasses until our eyes wavered, but saw no windmill. We made disparaging remarks about Lieutenant Tavera, now a deceased admiral, and wished he had studied treasure-map cartography from Robert Louis Stevenson."

A fruitless search for the windmill followed. The men of the Undersea Research Group decided to forget Lieutenant Tavera and his report and to search for the wreck as though they had no clues to its whereabouts at all.

The French divers returned to their ship, the *Elie Monnier,* to plan their strategy. All they knew was that the wreck was somewhere nearby, and that it lay in 127 feet of water. They cruised until they had reached water of the right depth.

Then they laid out a grid of steel wire covering 100,000 square feet, creating a pattern something like a football field on the bottom of the sea. The divers swam back and forth along the "line-markers," surveying the terrain. In Cousteau's words, "We would have found a watch dropped on the field. There was no Roman freighter in our web."

For five days they combed the bottom of the Mediterranean. To save energy, the divers were towed along from launches. Day succeeded day, with no wreck being found. On the sixth day, they were working some 220 yards from the spot Tavera had mentioned, when Tailliez suddenly surfaced, pulling his aqualung mouthpiece out to shout, "A column! I found a column!"

It was the Roman wreck, or what was left of it. As Tailliez wrote in his book, *To Hidden Depths,* "The sight was a thrilling one. All that remained of the Mahdia 'Galley' after two thousand years amounted to a collection of widely spaced lumps, with a number of columns arranged in four main rows. The general effect, in spite of the disturbance caused by the Greek divers, was overwhelmingly that of a ship, 36 feet wide by 120 long, lying on a north-south axis. Fragments of the ribs of the hull, of the deck, and of the keel were visible beneath the columns, or in the intervals between them."

Cousteau and Dumas went down in aqualungs the next day, after a champagne celebration the night of the discovery. Prowling through the mud of the bottom, the two skin divers examined the fifty-eight columns and the remnants of the ship, which had been twice the size of their own *Elie Monnier.*

Working in two-man teams, the Frenchmen explored the wreck. Because they had spent so much time merely finding it, they had only a limited time to do the actual exploration on the bottom. Each team remained on the bottom fifteen minutes at a time, the signal to return to the surface being rifleshots fired into the water.

The current that had so bothered Merlin's helmeted, suited divers was no problem at all to the free-swimming aqualungers. Unencumbered and agile, the men dug with their hands under the marble columns, clearing away the muck and passing cargo slings underneath. As the columns reached the surface, the colorful sea-creatures which had attached themselves to the marble withered and died in moments, and the explorers hosed the columns clean, exposing their whiteness to the hot sun. They brought up four complete columns in all, the biggest of them weighing more than three tons, along with fragments of other columns, two anchors that Merlin's men had ignored, and some bits of pottery. They also managed to bring up one of the ship's nails, and yard-long pieces of the ship's cedar ribs, still covered with the original varnish.

In the short span of time at their disposal, Cousteau and his colleagues were not able to make a thorough search of the site. But they had registered an important achievement all the same—the first major use of aqualung equipment in archaeological exploration. Since then, other archaeologists have explored the Mahdia wreck. Apparently it has not yet given up all its secrets. The mud still is a stumbling block for the explorers. Even the greater flexibility and freedom of SCUBA equipment does not solve the mud problem: whenever an underwater archaeologist attempts to probe the wreck, mud clouds keep him from seeing what he is doing.

But each season divers go down to investigate the wreck. The work begun by Alfred Merlin in 1908 is not yet complete. And, Captain Cousteau thinks, "Amidships there is unbreached cargo. I am certain that then as now the crew lived in the forecastle, the least desirable place of a ship, and that there are intimate possessions and tools buried there that could tell us about what kind of men sailed the Roman ship."

The sea holds many other treasures. Antikythera, Mahdia —the next name to go with those is that of Cape Artemision, in Greece, on the island of Euboea.

The first discovery in the Cape Artemision region was made in 1925. Evangelos Leonidas, a fisherman, was bringing in his net from the bay, and was stunned to find what looked like a man's corpse in the meshes. Black and swollen, it seemed to be the body of a drowned swimmer. The frightened Leonidas made the sign of the cross and muttered a prayer for the soul of the dead man.

Then he looked more carefully, and finally prodded the "corpse" with a cautious fingertip. To his relief, he found it was no corpse at all, but a bronze statue. He notified the authorities, who gave him a generous reward and took the statue to the museum in Athens. The statue was thickly encrusted with marine life, and it took eight months to clean it properly. Today, minus its barnacles, it is on display in Athens under the name of *The Ephebe of Athens*.

Other fishermen in the Euboea area heard about Leonidas' lucky find, and from then on started to examine the contents of their nets very carefully indeed. But, though Leonidas had received 300,000 drachma, then a considerable sum, the other fishermen felt that they could do better if they hid their finds from the authorities and secretly sold them to dealers in antiquities instead.

Beginning in 1926, small fragments of bronze statuary started turning up in the waters off Cape Artemision. The fishermen peddled these fragments quietly to the antiquities dealers, but soon Greek archaeologists knew what was going on, and the police moved in. The surreptitious trade in bronze fragments was stopped. An official expedition was mounted under the supervision of Professor George Karo, of the German Archaeological Institute in Athens. Alexander Benakis, a Greek art patron, contributed money for the expedition. The Greek Navy and sponge divers from Euboea did the actual diving.

Professor Karo had been particularly impressed with one fragment—the massive left arm of what was probably an important bronze statue. "We must find the rest of that statue," Karo declared.

The divers went down 600 feet off shore, in a strong current. It was not long before they found the statue from which the arm had come, and brought it to the surface. It was a statue of Zeus, the leader of the Greek gods. More than six feet tall, the statue is executed on an heroic scale, with the god's arm raised as if to hurl a thunderbolt. The majestic statue is considered by many to be the finest Greek bronze ever found. We have none that are older and few that are as outstanding artistically. The statue is in the Athens Museum today, but a cast of it, donated several years ago by the Greek government, can be seen in the main lobby of the United Nations building in New York City.

The great Zeus was not the only statue Dr. Karo's expedition found. Another, depicting a horse and its young rider, is unusual in its portrayal of the jockey's features. While most Greek sculpture is noble and rather remote, this unique piece showed a smiling, fun-filled boy evidently having a high old time with his horse.

Dr. Karo had problems with his divers, who were working at depths much greater than they were accustomed to. He had bought the latest in diving suits for them, but the divers laughed at the precautionary measures he insisted they take. It is dangerous, for instance, for a diver to come up from the depths too rapidly. Under high pressure, nitrogen is absorbed by the joints, muscles, and fatty tissue of the body. If a diver returns suddenly to the lower pressure at the surface, this nitrogen will escape rapidly into the blood stream and joints in the form of bubbles. Agonizing pain is the result, and very often death follows.

Divers have learned how to avoid "the bends," as this decompression disease is called. They rise from the water in slow stages, pausing along the way to allow the excess nitrogen to escape normally without forming the deadly bubbles. Decompression tables have been worked out in great detail so that a diver will know how fast he can safely return to the surface. For instance, a man who has spent twenty-five minutes on the bottom at a depth of one hundred feet must take four minutes to return to the surface, at the standard safety speed of twenty-five feet per minute. But a man who has spent an hour at the same depth must make two "decompression stops," of eighteen and sixteen minutes each, before he can come up.

Karo's divers, who had worked for years at lesser depths, where nitrogen absorption is not a problem, laughed at all his talk of decompression stops. One of them, to show how foolish he felt the whole business was, let himself come to the surface from a depth of 140 feet in one single rapid ascent. He climbed onto the deck of the ship, and laughed as the helpers unbolted his helmet. "You see," he might have been saying, "a diver does not need to worry about such things." And a moment later he fell dead as the nitrogen bubbles coursed through his blood stream.

The death of the diver cast a pall of gloom over the enterprise. The other divers, frightened now, became uneasy about going down at all. Since funds were running low, and since the expedition lacked the equipment needed for raising the rest of the treasure, Karo decided to call a halt.

Since that time, fishermen have found statues and other objects that almost certainly come from the same shipwreck off Cape Artemision. For example, on January 26, 1952, a fisherman named Soulitzes brought up three ancient vases. Another object, of great weight, broke through his net and dropped back into the sea.

Undoubtedly, there is still much to be discovered in the bay off Cape Artemision, and probably modern underwater archaeologists equipped with SCUBA will have an easier time of it than Karo's suited divers. The main part of the ship, with its other relics, is as yet untapped. There are so many sites to explore and not enough qualified explorers, that divers keep going on to new sites without fully exhausting the old ones. Before very long, surely, the remaining treasure will be discovered. Until then—as Dr. Karo remarked in 1928—"The rest of the treasure is quite safe, guarded for a better day in twenty fathoms of water."

Hundreds of other Greek and Roman ships lie in equal safety along the Mediterranean's bottom. In later chapters, we will see how Captain Cousteau and others have made use of modern underwater techniques to rescue these treasures of the past.

Before leaving the story of pre-aqualung underwater archaeology, it might be well to mention the last recorded instance of a ship laden with Greek statuary sinking in the Mediterranean—which happens also to be the very first instance of large-scale diving to recover sunken sculptures.

All this took place in the early years of the nineteenth century. Thomas Bruce, Earl of Elgin, the British Ambassador to the Ottoman Empire, had visited Greece and noticed the superb marble friezes ornamenting the great temple of the Parthenon at Athens. The Parthenon had suffered badly over the centuries, especially in 1687, when it had nearly been demolished after a lucky artillery shot landed in the midst of a supply of gunpowder that the Turks had stored there during a war with Venice.

Now, the Greeks were in rebellion against the Turks who had occupied their land so long, and Lord Elgin feared that the remains of the Parthenon would be destroyed in the fighting. So he arranged to purchase the friezes, panels, and statues of the Parthenon. While the Greeks watched in melancholy helplessness, the artistic treasures of Athens were trundled off and packed in sixteen enormous cases, and loaded aboard the *Mentor*, a brig bound for England.

The *Mentor's* westward course was almost the same as that of the Roman plunder ship, almost two thousand years earlier, that had gone down off Antikythera. And, the second night out, the *Mentor* befell the same fate. Passing

Cape Tainaron in a rising west wind, the brig was driven off course by a sudden shift in the wind direction. It began to ship water, and the Greek pilot decided to head for land until the storm subsided.

Passing north of Antikythera, the *Mentor* tried to land at that island's sister island, Kythera. As it approached shore, the crew dropped anchor. But the anchors failed to hold; the ship was driven into a jutting rock and went down in sixty feet of water.

Everyone on board escaped. But the cargo went down with the ship. There was the glorious sculpture of the Parthenon, rescued from the Turks only to sink immediately under the waves. Lord Elgin's secretary, W. H. Hamilton, who had been in charge of the consignment, now had the sad duty of informing his employer of the debacle.

Lord Elgin, in Constantinople, wrote back at once, telling Hamilton that he planned to salvage the sculpture. Poor Hamilton was ordered to remain on Kythera and guard the invaluable marbles until Lord Elgin's salvage crew could arrive.

Meanwhile the Greek war of independence began. The entire area became a hotbed of spies and intrigue. Russian naval officers, passing through, offered to salvage the wreck, but Hamilton decided not to let them try. An Italian hired by Lord Elgin tried and failed. Months went by, with the unfortunate Hamilton spending his time peering at the sea and probably cursing the day Lord Elgin had ever decided to buy the marbles.

Winter came, and still the wreck languished beneath the sea, and Lord Elgin had not been able to find anyone who could salvage it. Taking matters into his own hands, Hamilton left Kythera and hired some divers himself on the island of Samos.

This was some 150 years ago, of course, and so the divers went down naked, unaided by helmets or breathing pipes. Still, the Samian divers managed to do the job, descending for two or three minutes at a time. It took them two years. One by one, the big cases were hauled from the wreck and hoisted to the surface, and then deposited on the beach, to be carefully guarded. The *Times* of London commented:

"The lovers of the Arts, and the admirers of Classical Antiquity, will be exceedingly rejoiced to hear of this fortunate preservation of a collection made with so much care and judgment. It would have been indeed lamentable if, after they had escaped for so many years the ignorance and prejudice of the stupid Turks, they should have been lost on another element, just as they were on their way to a civilized country, able and ready to appreciate their excellencies, and whose artists are eager to ascend, by studying them, that height of refinement and perfection in sculpture, which so eminently characterized the efforts of the chisel in ancient Greece."

Lord Elgin spent a small fortune getting his statues out of Greece, and a good part of the sum he laid out went for the job of salvaging them from the sea. Still, he did not suffer any financial hardship. In 1816 he sold the entire group to the British Museum for a profit of about $150,000. The statues are still there today—somewhat the worse for wear, after 2500 years of ill treatment, but undeniably powerful even in their present multilated condition. Lord Elgin has won a kind of immortality, since the collection is know by the overall name of "The Elgin Marbles." And the people of Greece, feeling that they are quite capable nowadays of guarding their own treasures, have been asking for many years that the Elgin Marbles be returned to Athens. So far, the British Museum has turned a deaf ear. The many-generations-removed descendants of the Greeks of Plato's time must journey to London today to behold these glorious examples of their ancestors' art.

Chapter 3

The Oldest Statues
in the World

Nᴏᴛ all underwater archaeology takes place in the sea. There are caves, too, where men once lived and left evidence of their presence. Some of these caves are flooded. Then they become challenges to the boldest of explorers, who must make their way through absolute darkness and through bone-chilling pools to find the treasures of the past that they seek.

One of the greatest cave explorers of our time is a Frenchman named Norbert Casteret. He is not an archaeologist, but rather a "speleologist"—one who explores caves. Throughout a long life he has probed again and again into the black, mysterious caverns under the earth, bringing the light of scientific understanding to these realms of darkness.

Casteret's most exciting single adventure took place more than forty years ago, and was a venture not only in speleology but in underwater archaeology as well. Through a feat of bravery that made him world-famous overnight, Norbert Casteret penetrated a flooded cave and discovered the oldest statues known to man—prehistoric relics twenty thousand years old.

Casteret had begun his explorations before World War I, while a student in France. He wandered into grottoes and caves, driven by that intense curiosity which has impelled so many men of his type. "I do not know of an impression more absorbing," he wrote in 1924, "than that which one experiences on entering a grotto of whose mysterious, shadowy labyrinths one is ignorant, while drops of water, falling from the high vault, alone disturb the silence with their thousand little songs."

His particular interest was in finding the remains of the prehistoric men who had inhabited the many caverns of France in the dim past. He knew that the cave men had avoided the bigger caves, because of their fear of darkness

29

and of the unknown. They had dwelt in small grottoes, or in the entranceways of the larger ones.

World War I brought a halt to Casteret's early cave explorations. But when the war ended, he renewed his explorations. He visited the famous caves already discovered, with their striking prehistoric paintings and carvings. He studied the writings of the prehistorians who had discovered these caves. He explored caves of his own discovery, crawling through low passages, occasionally swimming in a chilly subterranean river.

In August, 1922, he reached the village of Montespan, in the Pyrenees. Caves in nearby villages had yielded a wealth of prehistoric carvings and paintings, but the grotto at Montespan had never been explored. Casteret was told that in dry weather it was possible to go about sixty-five yards into the cavern. Beyond that point the grotto ended in water, which touched the roof of the cavern. Did anything lie beyond the water, Casteret wondered?

"There is nothing," the townspeople told him. "The cavern ends. You will drown if you go further."

A famous cave paleontologist, Professor Jeannel, had had at look at the Montespan cave in 1914. He had entered the twelve-foot-high gallery, but had given up when he reached the pool of water that seemed to terminate the cave. There were no signs of human habitation, and Jeannel saw no reason to try to go further.

Stubbornly, Casteret decided to enter the cave anyway. After all, not far away in the cave of Tuc d'Audoubert, wonderful prehistoric statues had been found by a professor of prehistory, M. le Comte Begouen. On August 18, 1922, Casteret donned bathing trunks and entered the cave, carrying a candle.

To enter, he had to slip through a hole no bigger than his own body. He found himself in a long gallery, about a dozen feet wide, whose roof at times was only inches above his head. A cold, shallow stream ran along the bottom of the cave. When he had gone about 125 feet, the gallery made a right-angle turn and the ceiling dropped so low that he had to bend double in order to continue. And, going sixty feet further, Casteret found the water deepening until the roof of the cave met the surface of the subterranean stream. Here Professor Jeannel had turned back. But not Casteret.

"On arriving at this discouraging spot," he wrote, "memories of former explorations, and in particular that of the cave of Tuc d'Audoubert, caused me to decide that instead of immediately leaving the cave, as was natural under the circumstances, I would give myself over to reflection."

He considered the situation. The rock all about him was limestone, which is easily excavated by flowing water. Quite possibly an underground stream ran entirely through the mountain in which the cave was located—and this grotto, with its deepening stream, was the outlet for that underground river.

Casteret had another idea. He knew that when men had lived in caves like this one, twenty thousand years ago and more, the climate of this part of Europe had been quite different from what it is today. The weather had been sharp, cold, and dry, much like modern-day Lapland's climate. Suppose, Casteret asked himself, that the bed of the underground river had been dry during the cave-man epoch? Men might have lived in some chamber of the cavern thousands of years ago, and the stream could have risen again long after the cave men had departed.

"It was after having turned over in my mind these suppositions of so fragile a nature, but so tempting to a prehistorian," Casteret wrote, "that I resolved to venture farther into the vitals of the mountain and into the unknown reaches of this subterranean stream."

It was a reckless idea, as even he realized. Many kinds of danger lurked ahead. He might find the submerged channel continuing for many hundreds of yards. Or he might swim into a dead-end pocket and, in the darkness, be unable to find his way out of it before his breath ran out. He might become trapped in a tangle of branches, or caught in quicksand, or get hopelessly lost in the dark chambers of the cave.

Standing in icy, neck-deep water, Casteret considered these things, then decided to make the attempt anyway. Carefully he rested his candle on a ledge of the cavern. He filled his lungs with air—a strong swimmer, he could stay under water for two minutes at a stretch. Then, in the loneliness and utter silence of the cave, he dove forward into the water, one hand outstretched before him to protect him from jutting rocks, the other keeping in contact with the submerged roof of the cave.

He moved forward with care, feeling the contours and bumps of the roof, trying to memorize the shapes so that he could find his way back through the darkness. For a moment, it seemed that he would never emerge into air. Then, to his surprise and delight, he popped out of the

water and found himself breathing good air again. He had
come through the flooded tunnel that had seemed an im-
passable obstacle to all the others!

But, of course, he could not see a thing. Without pausing, Casteret drew a fresh breath and plunged back into
the water, returning to the outer grotto where he had left
his candle. He was overjoyed at this confirmation of his
guess. The cavern did extend into the mountain. But had
prehistoric men lived there? To discover that, he would
need a light.

The following day, Casteret returned to the cavern, once
again alone. This time he carried with him a rubber bathing
cap that contained matches and half a dozen candles. He
did not trust the unreliable flashlights of his day, and pre-
ferred the more old-fashioned source of light. Tightly closing
the bathing cap to keep its precious contents dry, he
plunged into the cavern at four in the afternoon and for
the second time swam through the flooded tunnel.

He emerged safely once again on the far side. Standing
in chin-deep water, he carefully took a dry candle from
his bathing cap and lit it. By the faint, flickering light, he
could see that the cavern extended far ahead of him. A
thin air space existed between the slimy cavern roof and
the surface of the underground stream. Holding his candle
aloft in one hand, the bathing cap in the other, Casteret
swam slowly forward into the darkness.

When he had gone four hundred feet, he found he
could touch bottom—cold, slippery clay. A moment later he
was clambering up a clay bank to the entrance to a large
room. Shivering from his icy swim, he tiptoed in.

The roof was thirty feet above his head. Great blocks of
stone had fallen from the ceiling, and the stream, now
shallow again, lost itself under these boulders. Fresh air
found its way down into this room from an air shaft somewhere overhead. Massive stalagmites of great beauty jutted
up from the damp floor of the great hall. But there was
still no sign that human beings had ever stood in this
majestic room before. Undaunted, Casteret crossed through
it, found the narrow channel of the stream, and continued
on. He was six hundred feet inside the cave. "Never," he
wrote, "had I experienced to such a degree the feelings of
isolation, of oppression, and of fear such as subterranean
surroundings inspire, where the most banal accident, such
as getting my matches wet, might prove fatal."

Leaving the great hall, Casteret rounded a huge pillar

that rose in the stream bed and found to his dismay that once again the cavern roof met the water. His way was blocked by a second flooded tunnel, and who knew how long this one might be?

Having come this far, Casteret was in no mood to turn back. Even though the water was deep, and "the vault bristling with black and pointed stalactites," he sucked in breath and dove beneath the surface. He swam for what seemed like an endless time, as this tunnel was much longer than the first. Finally, lungs all but bursting, he came up safely in a low-roofed air space. Now two flooded tunnels blocked him from the outside world. "The loneliness was tremendous; I struggled against an uneasiness slowly turning to anguish. I momentarily considered retreating: luckily the spot was unsuited to even the briefest reflection. Harried by cold and apprehension, I found I might as well go ahead as to retreat."

The gallery he was in now was so low that he had to crawl on all fours. Water dripping from the clammy ceiling put his candle out again and again. The rough walls cut him in a dozen places. At last, he reached another great hall, larger than the first. Huge boulders had fallen from the ceiling here too, indicating some convulsion of the earth in ages past. Casteret paused in this hall and danced a jig —not from elation but simply to restore the blood circulation in his cramped, chilled limbs. He wondered how much farther the cavern extended? Miles, perhaps? Would his supply of candles last long enough for him to make the return journey? Or would his excitement and curiosity carry him beyond the point of no return?

He scrambled over the fallen boulders in the great hall and once again entered the narrow, water-filled gallery. A dozen times he thought he had come to the end of the cave, only to find that another section lay beyond some giant pillar. Sometimes neck-deep in water, sometimes crawling along on a shelf of clay or pebbles, he forged onward, leaving footprints wherever he could as markers for the journey back.

Then the cave narrowed so much that his way was blocked. He could get his head and one arm through the opening, no more. Reaching in, he discovered a pool of water containing floating branches and a surprise—tadpoles! Casteret let out a whoop of triumph. He knew that tadpoles did not live in the depths of subterranean caverns. Therefore, he must have reached the very end of the passageway. The tadpole pool, no doubt, was only a few yards from the surface, on the far side of the mountain. Later, he learned that his guess was right.

Turning, now, he began the agonizing task of finding his way back to the mouth of the cave. From time to time there were numbing moments of doubt as to which direction he should take, but eventually he stumbled out safely. The longer of the two flooded tunnels had given him a nasty time on the way out; he had dived in at too steep an angle, failed to find the exit, and had to try a second time before coming through.

Casteret had two reasons for being excited over his five-hour, two-mile trip through the dank cavern. First, he had explored a hitherto unexplored cave, and that is always a special treat for a speleologist. And, secondly, on his hike through the cavern he had picked up the tooth of an animal—a prehistoric bison, *Bos primigenius*. Bison do not wander into caves on their own accord. Someone in prehistoric times had obviously killed a bison and dragged the carcass into the cave to consume it. The tooth was slim evidence of cave-man occupancy of the cave, but it was enough to fire Casteret's imagination.

In the days that followed he explored the cavern many times, finding new halls and galleries that he had missed on his first trip through. He found no further evidence of prehistoric man, however. And then a rainy spell flooded the cavern completely and forced him to abandon his quest for that year.

The following summer was one of the dryest that France had had in many years. Casteret returned to Montespan in August, 1923, bringing with him a companion, Henri Godin. The drought that year had lowered the water level in the cave so that it was possible for them to wade through the first of the two flooded tunnels with their candles still lighted. They passed through the first great hall. Instead of plunging into the second flooded tunnel, this time, they discovered a new, dry gallery to the left of the channel Casteret had explored in 1922.

This new gallery was 650 feet long, 16 feet wide, 13 feet high. Its appearance, Casteret wrote, was "fairylike." Trickling limestone and glistening stalactites covered its walls and roof. The floor consisted of bright yellow limestone slabs with scalloped edges, each upturned to form a basin of water. But the magical beauty of the gallery came to an abrupt end. They turned a corner and found themselves in a dark, dull passage with soil underfoot. The roof gradually dropped until for the final hundred feet they had to slither along on their bellies over the cold floor.

They emerged in another large room. Casteret decided to dig here for possible prehistoric artifacts. He lifted the small pick he had brought, and dug it into the cold, sticky clay.

After each blow, he had to scrape the clay off the pick with his fingers. Suddenly, as he was cleaning the pick, he felt a hard object embedded in the clay. "I knew I held one of those chipped flints which sometimes make the layman smile, but which delight any archaeologist."

It was a crude, almost shapeless piece of stone—but beyond a doubt it had been fashioned by the hand of an ancient man. Casteret handed the pick to Godin and told him to continue digging, while he himself looked around the gallery for other signs of man's presence.

Casteret knew that this gallery, so deep in the mountain, could not have been a dwelling-place. Cave men had not liked living so far from the light. But they had used the deeper, more inaccessible caves for their religious rites. Most of the great cave-paintings and carvings had been found deep within caverns.

By flickering candlelight Casteret prowled through the cave. Suddenly he stopped. The faint light showed him what was unmistakably a statue—the clay statue of a crouching bear, facing the entrance of the grotto. The bear, forty-three inches long and twenty-four inches high, stood on a pedestal in the posture of the Egyptian Sphinx. It was headless, and the calcite drippings covering the entire body proved that the sculptor had finished his work without shaping a head. The bear's paws were folded, with the right forepaw stretched out, the five claws plainly showing. Between the forepaws lay the calcite-covered skull of a bear cub. The clay statue showed the marks of at least thirty spear-thrusts. It seemed as though the statue had once been covered with the skin of a real bear, and that the huntsmen of long ago had staged some sort of religious ceremony that involved thrusting their spears into the clay statue. "The ceremonies which took place there in the bosom of the rock are almost nightmarish to imagine," Casteret wrote.

In breathless excitement the two men ranged the cave

searching for other prehistoric relics. They were found in abundance. Casteret pointed out horses modeled in relief, two large clay lions or tigers, and a number of sketches carved on the wall. "On all sides, carvings of animals, sketches, and mystic signs sprang to our gaze." Hyenas, wild goats, chamois, stags, bison, mammoths, horses, wild donkeys—all were depicted in rock carving with what Casteret termed "skill and striking realism." There were fifty pictures in all, and thirty clay statues, some of them badly damaged by the dripping water.

Continuing on into the next gallery, the two explorers found a horse's tooth, the skeleton of a small snake, and a footprint of a cave bear in the soft limestone, and more wall carvings. These included two horses that appeared to be pregnant, and on the shoulder of one horse was carved the image of a human hand with outspread fingers, as though to symbolize "man's domination over the animal world." Above the two horses was the carved head of a wild goat, and then—surrounded by strange wedge-shaped signs that Casteret thought resembled the cuneiform writing of ancient Mesopotamia—was seen "a curious human profile, round-headed, strong-nosed, with a wide-open eye, lidless and quite round, and a short beard."

Farther on, Casteret and Godin found human footprints in the clay, more carved flints, and the imprints of hands which had dug away the clay to form the statues. Animal claw-marks showed that beasts had been kept in the cave as well, perhaps to participate in some bloody sacrifice. Around a bend in the gallery, they came upon three large statues of lions or tigers, more than five feet in length, but badly damaged by time. On the wall near this group was a drawing of a mammoth, and near it more flint tools and bits of polished bone. Elsewhere in the cavern, Casteret found the bones of horses, bison, bear, and reindeer buried in the soil and clay, and then human remains, including an elbow bone.

It was indeed a museum of the distant past. Casteret wrote, "I shall never forget my awe at first seeing these marks, intact, after two hundred centuries of solitude. Such an experience repays in a moment all the hardships, risks, and countless disappointments which await those who would rob the jealous past of its secrets.

"A study of the art at Montespan indicates that this is a sanctuary, one of those sacred grottoes where the sorcerers of hunting tribes in the reindeer age performed their magic ceremonies."

Casteret and Godin, dazed by the wonders they had discovered, staggered out of the cave mouth and immediately notified several important experts on prehistory, who came to inspect the finds. Casteret's brother and other friends joined in the job of widening the outlet of the grotto. This increased the flow of the stream and lowered the water level so that it was now possible to reach the prehistoric gallery without having to duplicate Casteret's bold plunge into the water. The gallery at Montespan was declared a national monument. Its contents today rank with the most significant relics of prehistoric man ever found.

If Norbert Casteret had made his exploration of the Montespan cave thirty years later, much of his opportunity for heroism would not have existed. For he could have used skin diving equipment instead of the strength of his own powerful lungs to see him through the two flooded tunnels. The dangers of his adventure would have been reduced tremendously.

In 1922, of course, skin diving equipment did not exist, and it was clearly impossible for Casteret to have worn a diving suit in such cramped corridors. But, perhaps, even if Casteret had had an aqualung available back then, he might have disdained to use it. In 1954, Casteret, then fifty-eight, was part of a joint Anglo-French expedition into another cave in the Pyrenees, where once again flooded tunnels blocked the way. Ten of the twelve members of the expedition used skin diving apparatus, but Casteret did without it. As it turned out, the flooded tunnel had no apparent end, and the entire expedition, aqualungers and all, had to give up this time in defeat.

Despite Norbert Casteret's lack of interest in SCUBA, the new equipment has been of great value in cave exploration. One of the most active cave-diving organizations is the British Cave Diving Group, founded in 1946. These amateur archaeologists, who dive on weekends and vacations, prefer to use oxygen rebreathers instead of the more common aqualungs. The oxygen rebreathers are not safe at depths greater than thirty feet, but they have the advantage of being less bulky than compressed-air apparatus, and this is often important in the cramped confines of narrow cave corridors.

A section of the British Cave Diving Group in Somersetshire has been exploring a cavern called Wookey Hole, which had been inhabited for hundreds of years. Pre-SCUBA explorers in diving suits had found pottery fragments 2000 to 2500 years old in the cave. The British Cave Diving Group, excavating the sand banks in the cave with water jets, has found pots dating from the Roman occupation of Britain, human skulls, and even some glass bottles dating from the seventeenth century. This group of skilled divers has entered a dozen or more of Great Britain's submerged caves, and their activities are helping to uncover the archaeological secrets of their island's past. Beyond the archaeological value of their work, though, there is an element of sport that the divers find attractive. One British cave diver, Robert E. Davies, when asked why people enjoy risking their lives in dark, chilly caverns, answered, "It is obviously a dangerous, uncomfortable, and, to the uninitiated, an unrewarding sport. There have been some archaeological finds and some scientific data to be gleaned. But mostly it is the exploratory urge—like mountain climbing."

The "exploratory urge" has led men into caves all over the world. All too often tragedy has been the result, since not every cave explorer is as lucky or as skillful in avoiding danger as was Norbert Casteret. Even the famed Cousteau-Dumas-Tailliez team, probably the most experienced and most capable of skin divers, ran into trouble on a non-archaeological cave dive at Vaucluse, in France, and nearly lost their lives.

But still there are adventurous ones who seek out caves and enter them, sometimes simply for the sport and excitement of it, other times in the hope of finding archaeological treasure. Men have dwelt in caves since the beginning of mankind, and no doubt many unexplored caves contain relics of the past. Some of the greatest archaeological finds have been made in dry caves—the most notable one of recent times being, of course, the famous Dead Sea Scrolls which have given us so much new information about the Biblical age. Dry caves in China and Mongolia have also yielded much that is of value to archaeologists.

Many caves were never explored because water blocked the entrance. No one dared venture into such dark watery recesses, since the risks were too great, the rewards too un-

certain. Today, however, skin diving equipment tends to reduce much of the risk—and just how great the rewards can
be, in terms of archaeological value, is clear to all, ever
since the bold feat of Norbert Casteret showed the way in
1922.

Chapter 4

The Wine of Marcus Sestius

ABOUT the year 230 B.C. a ship sailed out of the Greek island port of Delos, birthplace of Apollo, bound for points west. The vessel was huge, her lead-plated decks capable of carrying tons of cargo. One huge mast rose amidships, bearing a sail made of bullhides sewn together.

The ship belonged to a Roman merchant named Marcus Sestius, who had left Rome to settle in Greece and go into the shipping business. In the year 240 B.C., Marcus Sestius had been made an honorary citizen of the island of Delos, which was one of the most important ports in the Mediterranean. He owned a fine villa in the district where the Roman merchants of Delos lived.

The cargo of Marcus Sestius' big ship was wine—wine from Greece, to be sold in the Greek colony of Massilia, which today is the French city of Marseille. Nowadays, shipping wine to France is something like shipping coals to Newcastle, since the world's best wine comes *from* France. But the French wine industry was just beginning, 2200 years ago. The Greek colonists who lived in Massilia had to import wine from their native land. The Massilia Greeks were rich, and liked wine, and would pay a good price for it. An amphora of wine was worth as much as a slave in Massilia.

An amphora of wine was the standard measure. An amphora was a big, fat-bellied earthenware jar that contained about six and one-half gallons. Amphorae were used to ship oil, grain, dates, olives, dyes, ores—anything that would easily go in and out of a jar—but most particularly they were used to ship wine. A full amphora of wine weighed about one hundred pounds.

In those days a ship was rated by the number of amphorae she could carry, rather than by her tonnage. Marcus

Sestius' ship was big, and was known as a "10,000-amphorae ship." The wine jars were stored under the main deck as the ship sailed out of Delos, because other goods were to be purchased along the way.

The ship of Marcus Sestius sailed westward through the Greek islands, which are close enough together so that the seaman is never out of sight of land for long. Then she left the friendly islands and embarked on the open expanses of the Ionian Sea, where land might not be sighted for weeks at a time. The cargo ship made the crossing of the Ionian Sea safely, and then passed through the Strait of Messina, which separates Italy and Sicily. The navigator of the wine ship brought his vessel unharmed past the dreaded rock of Scylla and the fierce whirlpool of Charybdis, which Homer, in the *Odyssey*, depicted as a pair of ravening monsters.

Up the coast of Italy the ship sailed, passing Naples, and dropping anchor at a port in the Gulf of Gaeta. Another Greek colony existed there, where pottery was turned out in great quantity for export. The merchants bought a considerable supply of black-varnished dishes and pots to be shipped on to Massilia, and stowed this new cargo belowdecks, with the amphorae of Greek wine. They also took on red wine produced near Rome, and stored the slender Roman amphorae three deep on the main deck. By the time the new cargo had been loaded aboard the ship, her decks were groaning, and her bow was dangerously close to the water. Perhaps some of the sailors noticed this, and muttered a curse. The greedy ship owners always loaded their vessels to the danger point. "We're carrying too much," the sailors must have said. "Why don't they have more sense?"

Overloaded or not, the ship sailed westward. Massilia was almost in sight when trouble struck. Perhaps a sudden storm blew up, or perhaps the vessel rammed a projecting knob of rock. Whatever the reason, she began to founder at a point now known as Grand Congloué, in the Mediterranean just off shore.

The great ship slipped below the waves, sinking keel first, her bow pointing eastward toward Greece. The stern of the ship, with the officers' quarters, was battered by the upjutting rock of Grand Congloué as the ship sank. She came to rest tipped on an angle, resting against the rock with her stern at a depth of 112 feet, her bow at a depth of 140 feet. On the way down, her anchor had become fouled on a ledge of rock sixty-five feet below the surface, and remained there.

What grief there must have been in Delos, when Marcus Sestius learned that his argosy had been lost at sea! What wailing, what tearing of hair, what gnashing of Roman teeth! But all to no avail. The gods had been unkind to Marcus Sestius. In a single day all his prosperity had been extinguished.

The creatures of the sea explored the sunken ship. Worms attacked her, but found it impossible to gnaw the wood, for lead sheathing, a sixteenth of an inch thick, protected the decks. Only later, when the sheathing had loosened, when its copper nails had begun to slacken their hold, could the worms begin their feast.

Sponges and sea urchins came to live on the wreck, which was fast being covered by mud and silt scoured from the limestone walls of the rock around her. Octopuses made broken amphorae their dwelling place. The wreck began to disappear under the coating of mud and sea creatures.

As the weight of the coating increased, the main deck, already burdened by its cargo, began to give way. Over the centuries the decks and hull yielded, until the main-deck cargo tumbled into the hold, and the Greek amphorae and Italian dishes burst through the ship's side into the depths. Then, possibly fifteen centuries after the ship had foundered, giant boulders broke loose from Grand Congloué, and toppled into the water. Thirty of them, the biggest weighing twelve tons, landed on the wreck. The water softened the impact of their landing, so that hardly any amphorae were broken. But the boulders helped to hide the wreck from sight. Eventually nothing was visible but a huge muddy mound on the bottom of the sea, a hill covering an area of ten thousand square feet. And here and there a few amphorae and some fragments of broken dishware poked their way up through the mud.

And so the wine of Marcus Sestius remained hidden on the sea bottom. Thousands of amphorae of wine, the oldest wine in the world, buried under two thousand years' accumulation of mud and shellfish!

A free-lance aqualung diver named Christianini was the first to come across the wreck of Marcus Sestius' wine ship. Christianini made his living browsing around on the sea floor off Marseille, picking up pieces of scrap metal that could be sold on shore. One day, Christianini stayed down too long and came up too fast. He doubled up, his legs paralyzed by the bends. He was rushed to the headquarters of the French Navy's Undersea Research Group at Toulon for emergency treatment.

There, the medics put the hapless diver into a steel chamber that duplicated the pressure on the sea bottom. Slowly they decompressed him, while the deadly nitrogen bubbles left his system. He survived, though his toes were amputated. He spent six months in the hospital at Toulon.

One of those who visited him at the hospital was Frederic Dumas, a civilian member of the Undersea Research Group, and a comrade of Captain Jacques-Yves Cousteau. The lonely, crippled diver was so grateful for Dumas' company that he said one day, "You know, Dumas, we divers never tell our secrets. But I won't be able to go down again, and I want to tell them to you."

The "secrets" Christianini wanted to impart dealt mostly with lobsters. It seemed that a colony of giant lobsters dwelt along the rock at the base of Grand Congloué. Some lucky diver, Christianini thought, could turn a handsome profit trapping those lobsters.

"How can I find them?" Dumas asked.

"It's easy. There's a natural stone arch a hundred feet down, off the western cape of the island. There's a place where a lot of old pots stick out of the mud. Just follow up above and you'll see the lobsters."

Dumas had no particular desire to make money trapping lobsters. But old pots sticking out of the mud? Could they be amphorae, maybe?

Amphorae would mean a sunken ship—possibly a big archaeological discovery. Dumas, in many earlier dives with Cousteau and Tailliez, had found amphorae on the sea bottom almost always a sign of a shipwreck. Greek and Roman wine ships had had a great deal of bad luck in the centuries before Christ, it seemed.

An expedition had been organized anyway. Cousteau and his companions had the use of their own research ship, the *Calypso*, and in the summer of 1952 they had been planning to explore a sunken ship known to exist off the uninhabited island of Maire, in the sea near Marseille. They decided to have a look at nearby Grand Congloué, while they were at it, and see if the "pots" Christianini had talked about were really there.

They set out for Grand Congloué in August, 1952. On board, along with the divers, was Professor Fernand Benoit, head of the Archaeological Museum of Marseille, to provide an expert opinion on anything that might be discovered. The *Calypso* moored off Grand Congloué, 10 miles off shore, a rock 500 feet long, 325 feet wide.

Dumas donned his aqualung equipment and went below. He had no trouble locating the limestone arch of which Christianini had spoken—but no pots, no lobsters. Had they been only figments of a sick man's imagination?

Cousteau went down. He intended to swim southward around the cape. Down he went, to a depth of 220 feet, but there was no trace of a wreck. Doubling back around the cape, he was just beginning to succumb to disappointment and irritation when he came across a single amphora at a depth of two hundred feet.

One amphora did not mean a wreck, of course; it might have fallen overboard in rough seas twenty centuries before. Cousteau stood it in the sand as a landmark, and began to ascend. He had been down a long time, at great depths. He could not remain at two hundred feet any longer.

On the way up, he stumbled across the wreck, at 140 feet. He saw Christianini's "pots"—dozens of amphora necks protruding from the mud—and dishes strewn around. But he had no time to explore; it was dangerous for him to remain even at this depth. Hurriedly grabbing up three wine cups and a corroded bronze boat hook, he continued on to the surface.

Professor Benoit was startled at the cups Cousteau handed him. He recognized them at once as Italian, dating from 200 to 400 B.C. He had excavated many cups just like them in the ancient Greek settlements in Provence.

All thought of exploring the Maire Island wreck vanished. They had found something here—something of great importance. According to Professor Benoit, the wreck was the oldest seagoing cargo ship that had been discovered up to that time.

Excitement reigned aboard the *Calypso* during the next few days. A corps of fifteen divers was aboard, and they went up and down continually, loading baskets with ancient pottery. The *Calypso* began to fill with hundreds of dishes and jars. The top of the mound had been skimmed clean, and the divers were now digging into the layers of mud.

But it seemed as hard as cement. Bare hands could not budge anything embedded in it. The amphorae would break when the divers tried to pull them free.

To add to the complications, the mistral descended two

months early that year. The mistral is a dry, fierce storm that sweeps down over Marseille and Toulon every autumn. In 1952 it struck in August. Gales turned the water foamy, and the *Calypso* bobbed like a cork in the water, straining at her leash. The divers, 140 feet down, were not bothered by the storm on the surface. But more than once, a basket of pottery carefully collected below would nearly drop back into the sea as the storm-tossed ship gave a sudden lurch. Moored to the rock the *Calypso* was in great danger of being dashed to pieces by a giant swell.

To protect the ship, Army engineers built a platform on the shore, and this platform was used as the base of operations. Equipment and machinery were transferred to it. A small house was built to serve as expedition headquarters.

To clean away the mud that covered the cargo, the explorers used a giant suction pump attached to an eighty-five-foot wooden boom on the island. Compressed air blasted away the encrusted mud, and the pump scooped up pottery and amphorae and piped them to the surface, where a filter basket separated out the mud and let sea water spill back at twelve gallons a minute. Two eagle-eyed archaeologists constantly watched the pump's output for valuable material.

Naturally, some of the pottery was broken by the pump. Down at 140 feet, the divers would operate the pump, aiming it at the horde of dishes and amphorae, and every now and then something would catch crosswise in the pump's nozzle. There was nothing to do in that case but smash the object with a hammer. At 140 feet, the divers could remain down only a short time safely, and there was no time to use finesse in unclogging the pipe. With at least fifteen thousand pieces of pottery in the wreck, the breakage of a handful did not matter.

Captain Cousteau has confessed one irresistible bit of vandalism that, perhaps, *did* matter. Of all the amphorae that came up from the depths, only one still had wine in it. About twenty were still sealed by an inner cork set in pitch, covered with *pozzuolana*, or volcanic mortar. However, all but one of these amphorae had holes drilled in their necks, as though the crewmen had been nipping wine on the sly. "Perhaps," Captain Cousteau has suggested, "that is why they sank!"

But one amphora was intact, contents and all. At that time it seemed to the members of the expedition that there would be many other filled amphorae, and so it could not be very serious if they opened this one. They broke the seal, therefore, and poured out about a quart of wine.

Cousteau and Ferdinand Lallemand, one of the expedition's archaeologists, poured glasses of wine for themselves and put them to their lips. Lallemand spit his wine out on the deck, but Cousteau, perhaps tougher, managed to swallow his. It was not a pleasant experience. Cousteau writes:

"I tasted all the mustiness and age there is in this world. The Greek wine had been dealcoholized, but it had no taste of salt. A poor vintage century, that wine.

"We have not found a second amphora with wine dregs in all the months since, after thousands of dives. There may not be another. We should have delivered the amphora, without breaking the seal and in an airtight bag, to a laboratory where the 2200-year-old wine could have been professionally analyzed."

The divers continued to go down, though the autumn storms increased in intensity. Cousteau's experiences in diving told him that each diver could work a seventeen-minute shift on the bottom without needing to halt for decompression stops on the way up. So each man did his seventeen-minute stint, with the sound of a rifleshot fired from above serving as his signal to surface. Coming up, at the standard safety speed of twenty-five feet per minute, took another five or six minutes. Each man was permitted only two or three shifts a day, since working in the dark, fifty-two-degree water 140 feet down was a strain on mind and body alike.

A minor mystery developed when it was noticed that many of the amphorae whose stoppers had been lost now contained pebbles, sea shells, and bits of broken pottery. Perhaps some of these fragments had been washed into the fallen amphorae by the action of the water—but they were also found in amphorae that were still upright. It would have been very difficult for pieces of pottery to have washed into an upright amphora.

The mystery was solved soon enough. Practically every amphora brought to the surface was found to contain an octopus! The many-legged creatures had settled down to keep house in the amphorae, and had drawn together barricades of pebbles and pottery to serve as "doors" for their dwellings!

The suction pipe yielded object after object—bronze knives, rings, hooks, dishes, bowls. Many fishermen's sinkers came up, most of them more recent than the wreck, lost over the centuries by fishermen casting their lines near Grand Congloué. As the divers dug deeper into the layers of mud covering the wreck, they began to find some of the Italian pottery with traces of the original varnish. Lallemand, the archaeologist, mentioned that he hoped they would be lucky enough to come across some dishes with the varnish still intact.

Dumas, an incorrigible practical joker, immediately obliged him. He covered one of the ancient bowls with black shoe polish and added it to a pile of pottery that Lallemand was examining. "Here it is!" Lallemand cried in glee as he came across the shining black bowl—but his jubilation turned to dismay as the polish came off on his hands.

Later on, Lallemand's wish was fulfilled. On the lower levels of the ship the divers found many thousands of the black Italian dishes with their glossy varnish untouched by time.

Tragedy nearly ended the expedition in its third month. Cousteau had hired two new divers, both men with combat experience underwater. One day in November, after a bad storm, the main buoy marking the site was moved five hundred yards out of position. One of the new divers, Pierre Servanti, volunteered to go down and see what had happened.

Servanti returned a short while later with the news that the buoy's chain had snapped under water. The anchor had disappeared. But the chain had dragged along the bottom, leaving a trail. Servanti suggested that if he followed the trail, he might be able to find the missing anchor.

Cousteau agreed to let Servanti go down again. "It's deep water," Cousteau warned him. "Take it easy. You probably can't find it in one dive." He gave Servanti a small buoy to take down with him. When he began to tire, Servanti was to leave the buoy as a marker so that another diver could continue the search for the anchor from the point where he left off.

Servanti dove in. But after ten minutes, the watchers aboard the *Calypso* no longer could see the trail of bubbles from the diver's aqualung. Immediately, one of the best divers in the group, burly Albert Falco, donned an aqualung and went down. He found Servanti, unconscious and white-faced, 210 feet down. Falco and two other divers brought Servanti to the surface, and he was placed in the ship's emergency recompression chamber while the *Calypso* sped for Marseille. But not even five hours of artificial

respiration in the big recompression chamber in Marseille
could save him. Servanti died that night. His undersea black-
out had been fatal.

Gloom descended on the expedition, and Cousteau considered calling a halt. But Servanti's friend, Raymond
Kientzy, asked that the work go on. They decided to continue. Cousteau himself found the anchor that had cost
Servanti his life.

In December, high winds battered the working platform
that had been built on Grand Congloué, sweeping many
bottles of compressed air and aqualungs into the sea. Working all night, the men were able to save the suction pump
and the eighty-five-foot boom from harm, and later they
were able to locate the articles that had been swept under.
But a new platform and headquarters had to be built. A
yellow tin house went up, containing beds for eight, and a
stone terrace that the divers decorated with amphorae. The
expedition remained in this shack all winter, bringing up
amphorae and dishes with what became monotonous regu-
larity.

Christmas passed, and then it was New Year's Eve. Four
months of work had gone by. During a New Year's Eve
party, one of the divers jokingly suggested that they bring
up the first amphora of 1953. The idea caught hold, and
at midnight a diving party braved the winter chill to
descend to the wreck for an amphora!

Winter ended. The sun once more beat warmly down
on Grand Congloué. Spring flowers blossomed on the bar-
ren rock. Lizards basked in the sun. And still the divers
went down. The number of amphorae that had been recovered mounted—1000, 1500, 2000. There seemed to be
no end of them. On May 15, 1953, the divers reached the
wooden keel of the ship. From its size, they realized that
the sunken vessel had been much larger than had originally been estimated. The number of amphorae might run
up into many thousands. As the digging continued, it became possible to work out some of the history of the ship
from the order of the cargo and from the types of amphorae
that were found.

The divers delighted in playing pranks on the archaeologists. One day Lallemand suggested that there might
be ancient coins in the wreck. Hoax-minded divers thought-
fully inserted a few modern aluminum five-franc pieces in
the suction tube to give Lallemand, watching the output
of the tube on shore, a moment of surprise. Another time

they sent up a small octopus that popped from the tube, alive and very much annoyed over the journey, right at the archaeologist's feet. A favorite amusement of the divers was to pretend to stub out a cigarette in one of the ancient dishes and watch the look of horror on the nearest archaeologist's face.

As they continued to dig into the western end of the wreck, the divers found marble dishes, blackened with smoke, which had probably been the crew's cooking utensils. They also found dozens of feet of lead pipe, three inches in diameter, with holes drilled for joints. The guess of the archaeologists is that this pipe was part of the plumbing system in the captain's quarters.

The ship's anchor, which had become separated from the ship as it sank, turned up later that spring, on a rock shelf sixty-five feet below the surface. The wooden parts of the anchor had long since rotted away, but the lead crossbar and collar remained, and the archaeologists were able to reconstruct its original design. Although modern anchors are weighted at the bottom, this ancient anchor was weighted at the top. As Captain Cousteau explains, "This was necessitated by the fact that the ancients did not have chain cable, but used rope on anchors. Rope might easily stretch taut in a wind and pull the anchor loose if it did not have a heavy weight at the top. Modern chain cable always hangs in a loop, even under heavy stress, so that the pull on an anchor is horizontal. Top weight is therefore unnecessary."

Salvaging the wooden parts of the ship posed problems for the divers. The ribs and timbers of the ship, fashioned skillfully from pine, cedar, and oak, seemed to be in good condition when examined on the bottom. But the wood felt rubbery to the touch. Two thousand years of ship-worms had dug their tunnels through it, eating as they went. Lifting large pieces of the fragile wood proved to be a complicated procedure. And when the wood got to the surface, it would shrink to a third its original size as it dried out.

In the early days of archaeology, many important objects were lost in this way because the archaeologists did not know how to preserve them. Any nineteenth-century account of excavation in Egypt or Mesopotamia will mention hundreds of times, "We discovered a fine copper pot (or wooden or bronze object) but it crumbled when exposed to the air." Today, chemical techniques for preserving fragile objects are employed by archaeologists. Plastics and other preservatives are used to save objects that would otherwise turn to powder a short while after their discovery. Sometimes these preservatives can be applied quickly with a spray, but often they must be laboriously applied with a brush, by hand.

Aside from pots and amphorae, the divers came up with thousands of lead-coated copper nails, with iron fittings and tools, and with strips of the deck's lead sheathing, all of which told the archaeologists much about the techniques of ship building three centuries before Christ. An interesting fact developed concerning the more than forty types of dishes, bowls, and pots that were recovered. Each type was of a standard design, with identical indentations around the sides. This meant that the pottery had been turned out in wooden molds, by mass production, instead of one at a time by hand. The dishes had been packed in an expert and very modern way as well. Although the wooden packing crates had deteriorated, the dishes were still stacked in their original patterns. Cup handles were stacked alternately at right angles, while small dishes were stacked within larger ones.

The pottery of Marcus Sestius' ship is of no great interest artistically. It is simple, cheaply made pottery without elegance or elaborate decoration. But finding a cache of such pottery almost in its original state has been of tremendous value to the archaeologists who are trying to reconstruct the small details of the life of the past.

The *Calypso* expedition encountered the same trouble that has hampered other underwater archaeological endeavors in the past: few divers are archaeologists, and few archaeologists are divers. Although Cousteau and his comrades had learned much about archaeology through experience, they were not really scholars by profession. There was always the chance that by ignorance or accident they might destroy some bit of evidence, trifling to them, that would have been of great value to archaeologists. But the archaeologists, 140 feet above the wreck, were unable to descend in aqualungs to supervise the excavation themselves, as archaeologists on the land always do.

Modern technology got around this problem. Closed-circuit television was used to let the archaeologists above see the actual site of the wreck!

Cousteau had experimented with underwater TV five years earlier, in 1948. But at that time video equipment was still too crude to serve the purpose. Now, though, with

an excavation of such importance going on, a major effort
was bent toward providing satisfactory equipment.

An electronics firm, the Thomson-Houston Company,
agreed to lend television cameras, cables, and expert tech-
nicians. A French engineer, Dr. Pierre Dratz, designed a
special wide-angle lens for underwater work, while Cousteau
and another engineer, André Laban, built a watertight housing for the camera. A loudspeaker in the housing, connected
to a microphone in a control room aboard the *Calypso,* en-
abled the archaeologists to communicate with the divers.

The camera and its housing weighed two hundred pounds
on dry land. But the air inside the housing buoyed it
up so that it would be weightless under water. The cables
leading from the ship to the camera were buoyed also
to remove their weight.

A diver named Yves Girault operated the camera on its
first test. He took it down to a depth of sixty-five feet
and transmitted views of jellyfish and the sea bottom to
the men on the surface. The camera worked!

Quickly they moved on to Grand Congloué and the
wreck. Another diver, Jean Delmas, took the camera down
to the 140-foot depth of the sunken vessel. He turned on
the two powerful six-thousand-watt bulbs, which cost ninety
dollars apiece and are good for only an hour's use. They
can be used only under water because of the great heat
they give off; on land, such bulbs would melt and explode
in half a minute.

Delmas descended, and the watchers on ship saw sea-
fans and rocks. When he was a hundred feet down one
of the engineers in the control room picked up the microphone and said, "Delmas, correct your focus!"

Delmas adjusted his focus and the image grew sharper.
The watchers now could behold the form of diver Raymond Kientzy operating the suction tube at the wreck site.
They said hello to Kientzy, who grinned and waved back
at them.

"Let's see that dish you're standing next to," someone
would say. And Kientzy would obligingly pick up the
dish and display it for the camera. Delmas then took the
camera to the sixty-five-foot level to give the archaeologists
their first look at the snagged anchor.

The television hookup was helpful to both divers and
archaeologists. The divers had the comfort of knowing that
an unblinking eye was watching them, so that if they got
into any difficulties on the sea bottom help would im-

mediately be dispatched. And the archaeologists, in the comfort of the dry cabin, were able to see with their own eyes the site of the vessel and to direct every stage of the excavation even more efficiently than if they had been at the bottom with the divers.

The friendly byplay between the divers and the archaeologists continued. A diver named Goiran kept jokingly telling Lallemand, the archaeologist, that "we divers don't see why we should risk our necks digging up these jars that you will hide in a museum. We're going to put the best stuff aside and sell it for a good price. Lallemand, how much will you pay for a big Grecian vase with beautiful pictures on it?"

Lallemand's answer was to lower a dollar bill in a bottle when Goiran had gone down.

But Goiran had a comeback. Soon afterward, when he was manning the camera and Lallemand was watching the TV screen, the screen suddenly showed a fine array of dishes that Goiran had set out on the bottom. Each dish bore a large price tag. Goiran pantomimed the expressions of an auctioneer trying to get Lallemand to bid for the pottery.

"The price is too high," Lallemand said laughingly.

Goiran shrugged and picked up a large hammer. He pretended to pulverize the dishes while Lallemand doubled up with amusement.

Sometimes the television equipment caused surprises for the divers. One of them, Jacques Ertaud, took the camera down without knowing it contained a loudspeaker. When someone spoke to him from the ship, he dropped the camera and headed hurriedly for the surface, thinking that the pressure had made him drunk. Then he realized where the weird voice had been coming from, and returned to get the camera.

Thousands of amphorae had come from the wreck, now, as well as vast quantities of Italian dishware. While the divers proceeded with the seemingly endless task of hauling the contents of the ship to the surface, the archaeologists busied themselves with a little detective work to uncover the history of the ship.

There were no skeletons in the wreck, and, of course, no documents about the voyage. But the archaeologists did have one clue. Stamped in the lip of the amphorae were the letters *SES*, sometimes followed by the symbol of an anchor, sometimes by the symbol of a trident. The archaeologists guessed that these letters might be an abbreviation of the shipowner's name.

Archaeologist Fernand Benoit knew from the shape of the pottery that the ship dated from the period 400–200 B.C. He then checked through the annals of Roman history until he came upon mention of an important and wealthy family of merchants named Sestius that had flourished during those centuries.

The writings of Livy, the Roman historian, mentioned one member of this family in particular, Marcus Sestius, who had left Rome to settle on the Greek island of Delos. Livy told how Marcus Sestius had been given honorary citizenship at Delos, and how he had built a splendid villa there. Since the amphorae had definitely come from Greece, and since Delos had been an important shipping center in the middle of the third century before Christ, and since the SES inscription seemed to link the amphorae to Marcus Sestius, all indications pointed to the fact that the ill-fated vessel had belonged to Marcus and had set out from Delos, stopping in Italy before going on to its doom near Massilia. Since Marcus had settled in Delos around 240 B.C., Professor Benoit guessed that the disastrous voyage had taken place about ten years later, around 230 B.C.

All this was guesswork, of course. But the evidence seemed strong in favor of Professor Benoit's theory.

During the summer of 1953, Cousteau and his men, growing a little bored with the by now dreary job of fetching amphorae from the muddy depths, decided to turn the project over to another group of divers and go off to Delos themselves, retracing the wine vessel's voyage in reverse, to search for some further information about Marcus Sestius. They left on the first anniversary of the start of work at Grand Congloué.

Heading southeast, they passed through the Strait of Messina, and stopped there and at the whirlpool of Charybdis to make underwater photographs. Then it was onward, as they crossed the once-fearsome Ionian Sea in a single night, and then into the Aegean Sea and to the isle of Delos.

Delos had once been a sacred city, where no sword was ever raised. Pilgrims from all over the ancient world came to worship there at Apollo's shrine. The wealth of Delos was great; traders of every race made it the headquarters for their shipping enterprises.

Today silt blocks the once-crowded harbor of Delos. So shallow has the water become that the *Calypso* was forced to anchor in the strait. The city itself was reduced to ruins. The troublesome King Mithridates, an enemy of Rome, had sacked Delos in 88 B.C., massacring twenty thousand Delians and carrying off much of the city's treasure. A pirate raid in 69 B.C. finished the job of ending the city's prosperity. Today Delos is a city of fallen columns and ruined, deserted villas.

French archaeologists have been at work on Delos since 1873. Most of the island's thirty-five residents today are members of the archaeological group. It was to the head of these archaeologists, Jean Marcadé, that Captain Cousteau turned for information about Marcus Sestius.

Marcadé let Cousteau look through the museum collection of thousands of fragments of amphorae, found in the city's ruins. Not one bore the *SES* trademark. Nor did a dozen unbroken amphorae, similar to those found at Grand Congloué, bear the markings of Marcus Sestius.

But then the archaeologist took the skin divers on a tour of the ruined city. Past broken columns and shattered temples they went, to the area where the rich Roman shipowners had lived. They entered the courtyard of one of the most handsome of the villas.

Mosaics on the floor showed patterns that suggested the sea, and even an amphora-shaped vase. Then one of the divers came across a mosaic showing a porpoise entwined with an anchor, an anchor very much like that on some of the *SES* amphorae. A moment later, another diver pointed to a second mosaic that portrayed a trident, similar to the one stamped on the amphorae. And still another member of the group, James Dugan, pointed out that the trident was in the shape of a Roman *E,* with two S-shaped brackets between the tines. *SES,* perhaps?

Guesswork still—but the guesses grow more convincing as the evidence mounts. We may never actually have proof that the ship wrecked off Grand Congloué belonged to Marcus Sestius of Delos, but certainly it would seem that way. And the archaeologist, Marcadé, offered one final clue. The handsome villa at Delos that contained the *SES* monogram had never been finished. Possibly, the loss of his big ship had thrown poor Marcus Sestius into bankruptcy, and he was forced to leave his villa incomplete!

Although Cousteau and his group turned their attention to other projects, work at Grand Congloué continued for several years. All told, some eight thousand amphorae were recovered, and no doubt several thousand more remain at the bottom. Enough amphorae and pottery dishes were recovered to stock all the museums of the world many times over.

The value of the Grand Congloué wine ship, though, lay more in what it told archaeologists about Greek shipping than in the hordes of amphorae it yielded. We know that the Greeks were energetic merchants and seamen, but they left few writings on the subject. Greek colonies all around the Mediterranean, in what now are France, Italy, and Spain, testify to the wide spread of Greek shipping.

But because the Greeks had not left any written information about their maritime industry, we had no real idea of what sort of ships they used, or where the main routes lay. The Grand Congloué ship proved that the Greeks had had vessels of unusually great size, as big as nineteenth-century frigates. And we have learned something about the trade routes, and how ships bound for the Greek colonies of western Europe stopped off in Italy to pick up cheap wine and mass-produced pottery for sale further west.

Archaeologists digging on shore have supplemented the findings of the skin divers. For instance, pieces of pottery bearing Marcus Sestius' *SES* trademark have been found far inland in Burgundy and Alsace. From this we know that Massilia served as the distribution point for goods coming from Greece, just as its present-day counterpart Marseille is the port of entry for much French commerce.

The quest for knowledge of the past is a difficult one. Archaeologists often must grope blindly in the dark. But, slowly and surely, they put together the scattered fragments of information, learning from an amphora here, a buried coin there, a bit of broken pottery somewhere else. The barriers of time are steadily being rolled back. First on land, and now in the sea as well, eager workers are probing the mysteries of the past. They are bringing light to the darkness that enfolds the world of the day before yesterday.

Chapter 5

The Sacred Well of the Mayas

BEFORE the Spanish conquistadors took possession of South and Central America, highly sophisticated Indian civilizations flourished there. In Peru, the Incas reigned; in northern Mexico, the blood-thirsty Aztecs. In Yucatán and what is now Guatemala and Honduras the race we call the Mayas held sway. Elsewhere, throughout Central and South America, smaller tribes developed their cultures—the Olmecs, the Mixtecs, the Toltecs, and many others.

The accomplishments of these peoples were extraordinary. They built mighty temples, excellent roads, imposing pyramids. Their sculpture was strange but beautiful in its fierce way. They worked precious stone like jade into fine ornaments and made shining jewelry from pure gold.

The Spaniards shattered these civilizations of the New World. In the name of Christianity—but really in the name of finding wealth—the conquistadors looted and plundered, killed and maimed. The Aztec king Montezuma, the Inca ruler Atahualpa, and the priests and learned men of all the different civilizations fell victim to Spanish greed. The Mayas, too, were conquered, and we do not even know the names of their leaders.

Neither the Incas nor the Aztecs nor the Mayas are gone from the face of the earth. Their blood still flows in the veins of thousands of Central American and Peruvian Indians, and in some remote places the old languages are still spoken. But the days of the great city-building cultures are over and dead. The Aztecs and Mayas of today are pitifully ignorant peasants who are often completely unaware of the great accomplishments of their ancestors.

For the jungle swallowed up the temples and pyramids. The achievements of the great Indian races of the Western Hemisphere were forgotten, dying out even in legend. The

Spanish had taken care to obliterate completely any trace of the intelligence and ability that had made the Aztecs, Incas, and Mayas great. Vines and creepers surrounded their awe-inspiring buildings.

In the nineteenth century, travelers began to come upon these jungle-swallowed monuments, and after their first amazed rapture they would begin to dig away the foliage to see the splendors beneath. In my book *Lost Cities and Vanished Civilizations* I told how a roving American, John Lloyd Stephens, found the Mayan city of Copán about 120 years ago, and how his account of the ruins there sparked an archaeological campaign to restore the Mayan cities that is still under way.

One of the greatest of the men who explored the Maya region was an American named Edward Herbert Thompson, born in New England in the latter part of the nineteenth century. It was Thompson who explored the sacred well of the Mayas and successfully carried out a pioneering exploit that stood for many years as the greatest single achievement in the history of underwater archaeology.

As a boy, E. H. Thompson was inquisitive, alert, and fascinated by the past. Roaming the woods near his home, he would frequently come across Indian arrowheads lying exposed on the ground. He formed a collection of them, and must often have wondered what the two continents of the Western Hemisphere were like in the days before the white man came to rule.

In his teens, Thompson came upon the marvelous book written by John Lloyd Stephens, entitled *Incidents of Travel in Central America, Chiapas, and Yucatán,* in which Stephens told of his adventures in the jungles of Central America and of his discovery of the forgotten and vine-covered Mayan cities. The book fired young Thompson's imagination. Hitherto, the only Indians he had known of were those of North America, relatively simple hunting and fishing folk whose only building materials were wood and hides. And here was Stephens, writing of vast stone cities in the jungle!

Could these city builders, Thompson wondered, be related to the North American Indians? He decided that it was impossible. Whoever had built the great cities of Central America had been some mighty race, wholly different from the red man of North America.

Who could these city builders be?

Thompson had an answer. His theory is one that no one

takes seriously today but which may yet turn out to have a germ of truth in it—though it seems too fantastic to be true. Thompson thought that the Mayas had been a surviving branch of the people of Atlantis, that mythical lost continent supposedly overwhelmed by the sea.

He put this notion forth in 1879, in a magazine article called "Atlantis Not a Myth." It was Thompson's contention that when Atlantis met with its downfall, its people, or some of them at any rate, escaped to the New World and built cities in what is now Mexico and Honduras.

It was certainly a bold and startling idea, and it attracted a great deal of attention in the United States. There was heated discussion pro and con. The man who had begun the discussion wanted nothing more than a chance to go to Central America, see these vast ruins with his own eyes, and explore them in hopes of finding some token that would prove or disprove his Atlantis theory.

Friends of Thompson helped him attain this goal. He was supported by the American Antiquarian Society and by the Peabody Museum of Harvard University. Through the sponsorship of these institutions, Thompson was able to secure an appointment as United States Consul in Yucatán. The fact that he went to Central America as a diplomatic traveler was an interesting parallel to the story of John Lloyd Stephens, who, some forty years earlier, had financed his own explorations of Maya-land by wangling a diplomatic appointment from President Martin Van Buren.

While preparing his Atlantis article, Thompson had come across an old book that held a special fascination for him. It was the *Relación de las Cosas de Yucatán,* written by Diego de Landa (1537–1579), the Bishop of Yucatán.

De Landa was one of those dedicated men of religion who came to the New World in the sixteenth century determined to bring Christianity to the savages, even if it meant killing any native who refused to accept the gentle teachings of Jesus. Diego de Landa saw no contradiction between Christ's word and his own often ruthless methods of obtaining converts.

De Landa felt that the best way of making Christians out of the Mayas was to destroy their pagan civilization. One of the ways he went about doing this was to gather together, in July, 1562, many of the Mayan books—writings on medicine, history, religious rites and ceremonies, astronomy, etc.—and burn them. "We collected all the native books we could find and burned them, much to the sorrow of the people, and caused them pain," de Landa wrote, with what sounds like great satisfaction at his deed. As a result of that act of destruction, only three Mayan books escaped to come down to us today, and the entire history and culture of this remarkable people was obliterated.

But de Landa was not entirely an enemy of knowledge. Though in religious zeal he had wiped out the precious literature of an entire nation, he managed to set down in manuscript form some details of Mayan life—their system of hieroglyphics and calendar-keeping, their customs, their way of life.

One section of de Landa's *Relación de las Cosas de Yucatán* (which means *Account of Things in Yucatán*) told of the city of Chichén Itzá, which contained a well into which the Maya priests had hurled sacrifices to their gods. De Landa wrote, "A wide and handsome roadway runs as far as the Well, which is about two stones' throws off. Into this Well they have had and still have the custom of throwing men alive as a sacrifice to their gods in time of drought, and they believed that they would not die, though they never saw them again. They also threw in many other things like precious stones and things they prized, and so if this country had possessed gold it would have been this Well that would have the greater part of it, so great is the devotion that the Indians show for it."

Edward Herbert Thompson may have felt a thrill of anticipation when he read Diego de Landa's account of the sacred well of Chichén Itzá. Perhaps, pouring over the old zealot's book, which had been lost for almost three hundred years and had only recently been rediscovered in a corner of the Royal Academy of History in Madrid, Thompson had some foreknowledge of the great exploit by which his name would forever be linked with that of the city of Chichén Itzá.

Chichén Itzá is located near the city of Meridá, built by the Spaniards after their conquest of Mexico. Today, the journey from the Spanish city to the Mayan ruin is a simple one, made each year by thousands of tourists. But when Edward Thompson made his first trip to Mexico, in 1885, it was a major project simply to reach Chichén Itzá.

He hired an Indian guide to take him from Meridá to Chichén Itzá. He had hoped it would be a short trip. He had been traveling for days, first by train, then by *volán,* which he called "that satanic contrivance which leaves one bruised and bumped from head to foot," and finally, when he was beyond the help of stagecoach transport, on horseback. Now, with his Indian guide, he set out from Meridá, which he thought would be close enough for him to visit frequently while he worked.

Darkness closed in on them as they moved slowly through the jungle, and the full moon rose. Still the horses plodded on, hour after hour. Thompson wrote, "Midnight passed and how many more hours I do not know, when I heard an exclamation in the vernacular, from my guide. Startled out of a half-conscious dream I came erect in the saddle.

"My Indian was earnestly pointing up and ahead. I raised my eyes and became electrically, tinglingly awake. There, high up, wraith-like in the waning moonlight, loomed what seemed a Grecian temple of colossal proportions, atop a great steep hill. So massive did it seem in the half-light of the approaching morning that I could think of it only as an impregnable fortress high above the sea, on some rocky, wave-dashed promontory. As this mass took clearer shape before me with each succeeding hoof-beat of my weary steed, it grew more and more huge. I felt an actual physical pain, as if my heart skipped a few beats and then raced to make up the loss."

Thompson was savoring his first view of the Great Pyramid at Chichén Itzá. Although his Indian guide immediately settled down to rest, Thompson felt he had to explore the pyramid right away. Breathless, he clambered to a rock ledge eighty feet above the ground, and stared at the forty-foot doorway of the pyramid's temple. "Is it to be wondered," he asked, "if my knees shook just a little and if I glanced apprehensively over my shoulder awaiting the terrible, majestic wrath of the god whose temple was profaned by the eyes of an unbeliever?"

Looking about him, he could see a dozen other pyramids and many buildings, ghostly white in the moonlight. Then he spied a broad, raised roadway, leading away from the temple, toward "a vast black pool overgrown with trees. Breathless, frozen to the spot, I could only look and look, for in a blinding flash I realized that I was gazing at the Sacred Way, and at its end the Sacred Well in whose murky depths even then might lie the pitiful bones of many once lovely maidens sacrificed to appease a grim god. What untold treasures this grisly well might hide! What tragedies had been enacted at its brink!"

In his own imagination, Thompson re-enacted those

tragedies. Staring into the murky water of the well, he pictured the priests, resplendent in their ceremonial costumes, advancing to the rim of the well, chanting their prayers, while the timid, fearful maiden approached the moment of her doom. He imagined how it was as the drums and prayers were silenced, and the rain god's sacrifice stood alone as the priest lit the sacred incense burners. Then the drums began a muted beat once again, and two powerful priests seized the terrified girl, advancing with her to the very edge of the well, holding her aloft, swinging her backward and forward to the rhythm of the drums, then letting her go, letting her hurtle far out into emptiness.

"Thus I imagined the sacrifice at the Sacred Well," wrote Thompson. "A sacrifice enacted not once but hundreds of times through many centuries. Thus it has been handed down in a dozen Maya legends and I wondered whether this grim old well really held at its far murky bottom the relics of ancient rites or, after all, the sacrifices were mere myths founded on some trial event, which grew and grew with each telling."

He had to find out. But how—with little money and no mechanical skill—was he going to get to the bottom of that supposedly bottomless well?

He knew it was going to be a formidable job. The well was wide and deep. It was stagnant now, its water slimy and thick with the debris of centuries of neglect. Tons of muck and rocks and leaves would have to be removed before a diver could go down.

There was nothing he could do just then, in 1885, but return to the United States and try to get backing for his exploration of the sacred well. But no one wanted to get involved in the project. He attended a scientific conference and told everyone who would listen about the archaeological treasures that undoubtedly reposed at the bottom of the well. They shrugged their shoulders. He went to his friends and tried to borrow money to finance an expedition. They shook their heads and laughed, in a goodhearted way.

"No person can go down into the unknown depths of that great water pit and expect to come out alive," they told him. "If you want to commit suicide, why not seek a less shocking way of doing it?"

Thompson was undaunted by their unwillingness to share his dream. If no one would back him, he would simply have to handle every aspect of the project himself.

He realized that there were three possible modes of attack on the well: draining, dredging, and diving. Some preliminary study showed him that draining the huge well was impracticable on his limited finances. Dredging, though, was a possibility—if he could get the necessary equipment.

Thompson went to Boston and studied with dredging engineers. He borrowed money and bought a stiff-legged derrick with a hand windlass, a thirty-foot swinging boom, and a steel bucket-scoop. Getting this equipment from the United States to Chichén Itzá was no mean feat. It was unloaded miles from his work-site and had to be transported piecemeal, "with only native assistance, without trucks or anything adequate on wheels, and over the poorest excuse for a road."

Once he had his dredge at the site, Thompson had to put it together. Many days of sweaty work were required, and time and again he was certain that the bulky, awkward thing would topple down on him before he could get it into operation.

It was impossible to dredge the entire well, nearly 190 feet across. Thompson searched for the most likely spot by fashioning dummies out of wood, of the size and shape of a human being, and hurling them into the water. Thus he found the spot where the sacrifices had probably landed. He began to dredge.

Thompson had hired a team of about thirty Indians to help him. He gave the signal, and his most trusted men began to swing the boom out over the well, and then to lower the steel bucket. It dropped beneath the surface of the green water and descended until it reached the bottom.

Carefully, the boom was swung back toward the brink of the well. Straining Indians turned the windlass, reeling in yards of wet cable before the bucket broke the surface. Wrote Thompson:

"Up and up it rose, until it was on a level with our heads; then it was swung in by the boom and lowered to the spot which I had selected, where every precious scoopful should be minutely and painstakingly examined on the sorting-tables I had erected. No treasure must slip through our hands; nothing must be damaged by careless handling. Anything perishable must be immediately treated with the preservatives which were ready and waiting.

"My hands trembled, in spite of my effort to control them, as I emptied the contents of the scoop upon the sorting-tables, for soon I must be either 'that clever chap who recovered the treasures from the Sacred Well in

Yucatán' or else the prize idiot of the whole Western Hemisphere."

Thompson examined the muck, spreading out every bit of it, and found nothing. There was no trace of anything remotely interesting. "It might just as well have come from any cesspool," he commented.

Again and again the dredge, its steel jaw gaping, swung out over the water, poised a moment, and glided under the surface. The workmen strained over the cables as it emerged, jaws tightly closed over debris. "And day after day," Thompson wrote, "I found nothing but ill-smelling rotted leaves and a few stones. . . . Sometimes whole trees were brought up and their weight made our steel cable sing like the string of a bass viol as the sodden mass was swung underneath the surface to free as much of it as possible and so reduce the weight before raising it clear of the water and dropping it again in another part of the pool where it sank with a splash and swirl of water."

Now and then skeletons of deer or of wild hogs would come up in the bucket, and once the skeletons of a jaguar and a cow, predator and victim who must have toppled together into the well. For days the dredge went up and down, up and down, interminably, bringing up muck and rocks, muck, more muck.

As Thompson tells it, "My high hopes dwindled to nothing and became less than nothing. . . . Doggedly I kept at it, however, determined not to stop until the absolute rock bottom of the well was reached. I tried not to let my Indians see that I was discouraged, but they did see it nevertheless, and I think wondered every day how much longer the crazy stranger would persist in his foolishness and pay them high wages for bringing up mud, useless even as fertilizer, from the bottom of an abandoned well."

Thompson became depressed. "Is it possible," he asked himself, "that I have let my friends in for all this expense and exposed myself to a world of ridicule only to prove what many have contended, that these traditions are simply old tales, tales without any foundation in fact?"

On a bleak, rainy, discouraging day, the dredge came up with what looked like a pair of ostrich eggs, cream-colored against the black mud. They were of some resinous substance. Thompson sniffed them, cautiously nibbled one, then had the lucky idea of holding one over a flame. A fragrant perfume spread through the air. He had found copal—Mayan incense!

"That night for the first time in weeks," he wrote, "I slept soundly and long."

The dredge had finally burrowed through the accumulated muck of the past four hundred years and had reached the layer of Mayan deposits. From that time on, hardly ever did the dredge emerge with nothing significant in it. More balls of incense came up, and the rotted baskets that had once contained them. A wooden knife, arrowheads, bits of pottery, spear points, copper disks, bells, jade fragments, rubber balls and figurines, obsidian knives. Thompson was amused to discover that some of the Mayas had cheated a little when making their offerings to the gods. A few of the incense balls were not solid throughout, but were filled in the center with leaves, sticks, and rubbish—a cheap substitute for solid incense. Perhaps it had been thought the gods would never notice!

Then, one day, a skull came up, bleached and polished to gleaming whiteness. Examination showed it to be that of a young girl, confirming Bishop de Landa's tale of human sacrifice. Then a pair of dainty sandals rose from the muddy depths, and more skeletons—most of them of girls, but now and then the skeleton of a man, with broad shoulders, thick skull, a heavy frame. Perhaps warriors had been sacrificed as well as maidens. But later examinations showed that these male skeletons were those of old men. Had one of the terrified girls pulled a priest into the water with her? Perhaps.

For months, archaeological treasures came from the deep. There were objects of gold, now, particularly small golden bells that had been flattened with a mallet before they were thrown into the water. Many of the jade ornaments had been snapped in half—as though they had had to be "killed" before the rain god would accept them. "The treasure of Chichén Itzá was not valuable in terms of money," Thompson wrote, "but its archaeological value was enormous."

Thompson began to realize, though, that he was approaching the limits of what could be done by dredging. The bucket was starting to bring up splinters of limestone, indicating that bottom had been reached. Yet much of the well was beyond the dredge's grasp.

A great deal had been found already—ninety skeletons and a huge collection of archaeological treasures. "I could not quarrel with our good fortune thus far," Thompson wrote. "I felt well repaid, even if we should discover nothing else, for all my effort and expense. My highly speculative venture had amply justified itself. I had proved conclusively the history of the Sacred Well.

"But our dredging operations, together with soundings made from time to time, indicated clearly that the bottom of the well was very uneven—a series of hummocks; almost a miniature mountain range. And in the pockets between those hummocks, where our dredge could not reach, might there not be other treasures?—objects heavier and smaller in size than anything we had yet found; things which, because of their weight, would sink through the mud to the very bottom of the well?"

Thompson kept dredging until nothing more could be accomplished through that method. Now, he saw, it was time for the operation to enter a second phase—to go on to actual diving, and enter the well in diving suits to recover the smaller treasures that had escaped the dredge's jaws. "What could be more interesting, more romantic," Thompson asked, "than to go down under sixty feet of water to the very bottom of that grim pit?—to tread the corridors of the most sacred and abysmal abode of the Rain God?"

It was an audacious plan. The twentieth century was only a few years old, and the era of aqualungs was far in the future. Thompson's self-imposed task involved going down to great depths and working in total darkness at a temperature only a little above freezing.

He was prepared for his bold exploit, though. In the years past, he had become an experienced deep-sea diver. His experience, though, had been gathered in open, clear water. Now, he was planning to descend into opaque depths confined by high-rising cliff walls, and made dangerous by huge vines twisting and turning like great serpents.

To assist him, Thompson hired two Greeks, professional divers who had been harvesting sponges off the coast of Florida. The diving suits to be used were made of rubber-lined canvas with big copper helmets, cloth-lined and with glassed goggle eyes. Lead plates slung around the neck and metal-soled boots were used to aid in the descent. Hoses linked the divers with their breathing supply on the surface.

Thompson and one of his Greeks suited up, while the other remained on shore to run the equipment. Thompson was the first to go down, in his words "clambering down the rope ladder about as gracefully as a turtle falling off a log."

Down he went. He automatically checked to see that

his air line and life line were free and clear of obstacles. At a depth of ten feet, he found himself in complete darkness. Air pressure made his ears ache until he opened his helmet valves, equalizing the pressure. Down, down, down. He wrote, "I felt . . . a strange thrill when I realized that I was the only living being who had ever reached this place alive and expected to leave it again still living. Then the Greek diver came down beside me and we shook hands."

Thompson had purchased the latest and best underwater searchlight available. But so muddy, so dark was the water that the lights were useless. They had to work by their sense of touch alone, using their gloved fingers to probe through the mud.

Although they had brought an underwater telephone to the bottom of the well with them, they rarely bothered to use it. A few tugs on the signal rope were sufficient for communication with topside. When Thompson and his Greek diver wanted to speak to each other, they could do so by touching the metal fronts of their helmets together to conduct the sounds.

Their teeth chattered constantly. When they came up, after each two-hour diving session, their lips were blue and their bodies goose-fleshed from the intense cold, and steaming hot coffee was always the first order of business.

Working at sixty feet, they were under considerable pressure. But the pressure of air in the diving suit offset this, so that when at the bottom they seemed to have no weight at all, despite the lead plates around their necks and the two-inch lead soles on their boots. As a result, even the slightest stamp of a foot against the bottom could send them soaring.

Thompson was careful most of the time. But once, fascinated by the finds he was making, he carelessly forgot to let the excess air out of his diving suit before surfacing. He stamped his foot to rise and promptly turned feet-uppermost because of his buoyancy. He sped to the surface, his metal soles striking the hull of the diving boat with a resounding thump. The Indians aboard the boat were terrified at the sound and even more appalled when they realized what had caused it. But Thompson quickly surfaced and opened his helmet valves.

"God be praised, he is laughing!" shouted Juan Mis, his Indian foreman, and the incident ended without serious consequences.

One of the chief aims of the diving work was to discover the nature of certain large, smooth stone objects that had occasionally been found by the dredge, only to slip through the jaws of the bucket. Groping along the bottom, Thompson found these stones and fastened chains around them. The derrick of the dredge was used to lift them to the surface. Some bore hieroglyphic carvings, while others were statues. One huge stone was a perfectly sculptured statue of a seated god or priest which reminded Thompson of Rodin's "The Thinker."

On a later dive, Thompson searched for small objects that were buried in the silt along the humps and crevices of the bottom. He came upon small objects that to his gloved hands felt like coins, and after collecting about thirty of them, his curiosity got the best of him and he came to the surface. Even before he had unsuited, he opened his pouch and poured out a wonderful treasure of little objects:

"Beautiful embossed rings, small bells of copper, several bells of pure gold. . . . There were bells and ornaments, and medallions of gold repoussé and gold filagree, of exquisite design and craftsmanship. There were lovely carved jade beads and other objects of jade. Just as truly as any mining prospector, I had struck gold, but gold tremendously more valuable than his raw nuggets; for, whatever might be the mere intrinsic value of my golden finds, each bit was in reality beyond price."

It was only the beginning. A vast horde of Mayan treasure emerged. The gold value alone would have been hundreds of thousands of dollars, had the little bells and rings simply been melted down. One single day saw two hundred of the small golden bells recovered. Thompson showed them to the Indians, who stared in wonder and awe at *los cascabeles de los antiquas*, the bells of the ancient people.

More and more and more came from the well as the diving continued. For hundreds of years, the Mayas had hurled objects into the well, and Thompson, dazzled by the profusion, was bringing up an incredible quantity of material.

One day a handful of small copper masks, about an inch long and half an inch wide, were found. Oddly, they were discovered on the same day of a modern native carnival at which everyone wears masks. Thompson's Indian helpers quite seriously speculated that the rain god, Yum Chac, had sent the masks up in recognition that it was carnival day. Thompson noted the strange fact that neither before nor after that day were such masks ever found in the well.

Then came chisels, flint knives with handles of gold, statuettes, more bells, more jade. One day three Americans, one of them an archaeologist from Harvard, came to visit Thompson, and they watched the operation. Thompson was using the dredge again that day, and when one load came up, a gray, dreary-looking object was seen to be dangling from the fangs of the bucket.

"It must be one of the rain god's old shoes," laughed one of Thompson's visitors.

But then the bucket swung around, and they had a clearer view of the object. It was a large copper disk, covered with engravings of the sun god. Thompson and his visitors watched tensely as the bucket approached the shore, while the "old shoe," now seen to be an object of wonderful artistry, teetered and threatened to drop back into the well. At last Thompson's eager hands gathered it in—one of the finest of all his recovered Mayan treasures.

Later, other similar disks came up, some of copper, others of gold. "Every day was literally a golden day," wrote Thompson. One golden bowl was nine inches in diameter, others only slightly smaller, and there were twelve plain disks of gold, evidently originally intended to bear designs like all the others, but for some reason thrown blank into the well.

The total yield of the sacred well was enormous. Here are some excerpts from the list compiled by Thompson's friend, T. A. Willard:

"One basin of fine gold, twelve inches in diameter with shallow rounding bottom. About a pound in weight.

"Four other basins, bowls or cups, smaller in size, uncarved, but of massive material and very artistic in contour.

"Seven gold disks, embossed or beaten, about ten inches in diameter.

"Eight gold disks, embossed or beaten, about eight inches in diameter. . . .

"Ten human or monkey-like figures of gold.

"Twenty gold rings, mostly of thin but pure gold.

"Eleven reptile and animal figures, probably brooches and similar ornaments; all massive gold and finely worked. Frogs, bat-like figures and monkey-like objects, most of them cast (not beaten work), massive and of pure gold.

"Fourteen jade globes, one and a half inches in diameter, all very finely polished and several finely carved with well-executed figures and other designs.

"Many beautiful flint spearheads worth many times their weight in gold, worked down to the thickness of a steel spearhead with edges as sharp as a razor, the finest ever found anywhere in the world.

"One solid-gold mask seven inches in diameter, the eyes closed as if in sleep or in death and over the right eyelid the same kind of slanting cross that we often see carved on the so-called elephants' trunks.

"A thousand other articles of great value to archaeology."

The archaeological treasures Thompson found were given to the Peabody Museum of Harvard University. But the government of Mexico, in later years, was distressed by the way these important historical relics had been carried off, by a foreigner, to a foreign land. This is another standard headache for the archaeologist: most important archaeological material lies buried in backward countries where the people are unable or unwilling to excavate themselves, but resentful when outsiders do the job. In the nineteenth century, the early archaeologists were often forced literally to work secretly, lest the governments of the countries where they were digging find out about their activities and confiscate their hoard.

Today these conflicts are avoided in advance. When an expedition comes from one country to dig in another, an agreement is reached ahead of time about the disposition of the treasures that might be found. Sometimes the archaeologists agree to give half of what they find to the country in question. Sometimes, they agree to turn over everything, in return for the right to study it in the country's museums.

Thompson, in the early years of this century, simply carried off what he found. Mexico was in a state of political chaos then, and it would have been impossible to negotiate any such agreements with anyone. Despite some public indignation over Thompson's acts, the Supreme Court of Mexico ruled that he had not broken any Mexican laws of the time. Even so, the Peabody Museum voluntarily presented ninety-four of Thompson's discoveries to the Mexican National Institute of Anthropology and History in 1960.

Chapter 6

More Treasure from Maya-Land

EDWARD HERBERT THOMPSON explored the Sacred Well of Chichén Itzá from 1904 to 1907. As we saw in the previous chapter, the treasure he drew from the well was enormous, and his work will stand forever as one of the landmarks of archaeology.

But Thompson knew that he had not exhausted the contents of the well—had not even begun to tap the treasure of Chichén Itzá. His pioneering work had been carried out at a time when equipment was crude and diving a difficult task. His blind groping in the muddy darkness, though it had yielded much, certainly could not have accounted for every object thrown into the well during the time it was in use as a sacrificial repository—a period which may have been five hundred to a thousand years in length.

"With all the precious objects I have taken by force from the Rain God," Thompson wrote, "I am very sure that I have wrested from him not a tenth of his jealously held treasure. There are many, many more golden ornaments hid away in the recesses of the uneven floor of the pit, and many, many things even more priceless than gold to the antiquarian."

Thompson remained in Mexico almost to the end of his long life, and carried out many other feats of archaeological endeavor until his death in 1935. A few years before his death, he took this prophetic glance into the future of Mayan archaeology:

"All this (the further exploration of the Sacred Well) I leave to the engineer of a future day—and I say engineer advisedly, for it is going to be an engineering task to strip the old well of all it holds. It will first have to be dredged over its whole area, not with the crude hand-operated device which I have used, but with more powerful and modern, mechanically operated equipment. Then a huge, specially designed diving-bell will be required, so that men may work under it quite protected from the water and with ample illumination."

Thompson was right that some day archaeologists would return to the sacred well. But the "specially designed diving-bell" that he thought would be required proved to be unnecessary. The development of the aqualung, only a few years after the great old archaeologist's death, made possible an exploration of the sacred well of Chichén Itzá such as Thompson could never have imagined would ever take place.

The new expedition was formed thanks to a rising spirit of nationalism among Mexican archaeologists. Untold treasures had come from the sacred well, but where were they?

Were they in Mexico? No!

They were in the Peabody Museum of Harvard, thousands of miles from Mexico. Even the ninety-four objects that the Peabody Museum had given to Mexico in 1960 did not begin to soothe the hurt.

Imagine the outcry there would be in the United States if a group of, say, Belgian archaeologists went to New England and proceeded to unearth hitherto unknown relics of the Pilgrim Fathers—and then carried away all that they had found to some museum in Brussels! The whole nation would be up in arms. Congress would demand an investigation. Historians would object that a vital segment of American history had been taken from the country.

Of course, nothing of this sort could really happen today, in America or almost anywhere else. Foreign archaeologists no longer simply descend on a country and begin to dig. Everything must be cleared well in advance.

However, this did not help the Mexicans. Thompson's work had been done long ago, and could not be undone. And Mexico was still lacking any important collection of objects from the sacred well, or *cenote*. And, several years ago, a group of Mexicans decided to re-explore the *cenote* at Chichén Itzá. After all, they pointed out, Thompson had used primitive equipment, and must have left a great deal of material still in the well. Modern equipment would be able to locate the remaining objects, and this time they would remain in Mexico. "We can give our country its own collection," declared Pablo Bush Romero, who was the president of a group called The Exploration and Water Sports Club of Mexico—known by its initials in Spanish as CEDAM.

CEDAM was made up of a number of skilled skin divers who found the hobby an enjoyable one. It did not include any archaeologists among its members, though like many skin divers they had an amateur interest in what might be found beneath the surface of such archaeological treasure-troves as the Chichén Itzá *cenote*. Some of the members had taken part in archaeological expeditions elsewhere in the region, and had explored sunken ships in the Caribbean.

Chichén Itzá, though, offered special difficulties. The water of the well is muddy and murky. Skin divers would have a hard time seeing anything of small size in the clouded water. By themselves, divers might explore the well, but some efficient means was needed to bring any artifacts to the surface.

The CEDAM people took their problem to George M. Clark, head of the Yucatán Exploring Society. Mr. Clark suggested using the Link air-lift, which in a brief time had established itself as one of the most valuable tools of the underwater archaeologist.

The air-lift was invented by Edwin Link, famous as the inventor of the Link Trainer used in teaching aviation cadets how to fly. Link, an undersea explorer himself, designed his air-lift for use in exploring the sunken city of Port Royal, Jamaica. The Link air-lift consists of a pipe, about ten inches in diameter, through which small objects are sucked from the ocean bottom by a blast of compressed air, and spouted up onto shore or onto the deck of a boat.

An expedition to Chichén Itzá was organized, supported by funds from the National Geographic Society, which sponsors much work of this sort. The air-lift was to be used to supplement the work of divers from CEDAM and the Mexican navy, and trained archaeologists would be on hand to supervise the recovery of the objects from the *cenote*.

The first step was to install a derrick on the brink of the cliff, to lower equipment into the well. Then the divers' barge, a platform eight feet by twelve, was carefully lowered the nearly eighty feet to the water's surface. Not only equipment but divers as well had to be lowered by derrick, since the sheer walls of the *cenote* could not be scaled.

The divers paused on the small barge, staring into the murky depths of the well where, five hundred years ago, the Mayan priests had hurled their sacrificial victims. Not since 1907, and E. H. Thompson, had anyone ventured into the dark waters of the well. Donning their aqua-lungs, the divers slipped into the water. One of them, a

Mexican motion-picture producer named Genaro Hurtado, was clad in a weird looking diving suit with a hood and painted scales. It was left over from his last movie, called *Monster of the Deep*. The other divers wore more conventional suits.

As one of them, a photographer named Bates Littlehales, describes the experience, "The whole setting was eerie: the water seemed to have turned to ink. With my underwater flashlight, I couldn't see beyond my arm. Hearing only my own breathing, I moved hand over hand, following a line down 40 feet to the rock anchor. By touch, I established the shapes of fallen boulders and twisted, waterlogged trees. As mud churned up from the bottom, my light became useless."

The early dives were made simply to familiarize the expedition with the contours of the well bottom, and not to find archaeological treasure. The divers asked each other what they would most like to find in the well.

"A complete skeleton wearing jewelry," said Laverne Pederson. He was filming the expedition for the American Broadcasting Company and wanted something spectacular to record.

"A sacrificial knife," three of the other divers said. They knew that the Mayan priests had sometimes sliced out their victims' hearts before throwing them into the well.

Other members of the expedition had even more fanciful requests. Bates Littlehales hoped to find a full set of Spanish armor, which might mean that one of the Spaniards had been thrust into the well during the conquest of the Mayaland. Archaeologist William Folan wishfully dreamed of discovering Mayan hieroglyphic records in the well. But Ponciano Salazar, the director of the expedition, had the most reasonable wish of all.

"I would like merely to find something Thompson did not find," he said.

After the exploratory dives had provided a fairly good idea of the underwater topography of the well, it was time to bring the air-lift into play. For this, a larger raft had to be lowered into the well. Steel drums kept it afloat, and it had a hole in the center for the air-lift pipe. The members of the expedition set up a sieve of wire around the pipe mouth. This "strainer" would catch any artifacts that emerged from the well, while letting water and mud fall back.

As they worked to install the air-lift, an old man came to visit the site. He had the hooked nose and sharp cheekbones of the pure-blooded Maya, and spoke the Maya language. "I worked here when Señor Thompson dredged," he said. And he told the party that Thompson had done his work in a different part of the well.

That was good news. Perhaps the air-lift would bring up treasures that Thompson had not even approached. Excitement ran high.

The air-lift was turned on. One end emerged on the raft; the other, thirty feet down in the dark water, would be guided by divers. The pump rumbled into life. Water spouted high onto the sieve. Bits of wood, small pebbles landed on the wire screen. The watchers held their breaths.

"Copal!" someone shouted.

It was the first discovery. Copal was a resin that the Mayas had used as incense in their religious ceremonies. Thompson had found hundreds of these incense balls.

More of them followed now. Fragments of pottery spurted onto the screen, then a ceramic bowl. A few moments later came a rubbery statuette twelve inches long—a Mayan idol. The air-lift was yielding important material, now. Thompson had by no means exhausted the contents of the sacrificial well in his four years of dredging.

It was impossible, though, to take any underwater photographs. The murkiness of the water hid every detail of the well floor.

The treasures turned up by the air-lift more than made up for this misfortune, though. Deeper and deeper the tube went, stirring up layers of mud that had not been disturbed since the time of Christopher Columbus and even earlier. More copal, sometimes pressed into ceramic incense burners; countless beads; bits of polished jade; pottery whole and in fragments. The archaeologists were kept busy on the barge, snatching their treasures from the stones and mud that also were spewed up.

After a month's work, the first wooden figure came to light—a crude but powerfully carved idol, perhaps of the rain god Chac. It was an important find, but on the same day one of the divers made a sacrifice of his own to the gods of the well when he lost his expensive Rolex wristwatch in the murky depths.

They repeated Thompson's experience of finding hundreds of little bells. Some of them were of copper, a few bore traces of gold. Hardly any of the bells had clappers. The Mayan priests had "killed" every object thrown into the well, silencing bells by removing their clappers, and damaging jade statuettes or ceramic idols.

There were also plenty of less ancient objects recovered. Chichén Itzá has been one of Mexico's chief tourist attractions for more than forty years, and apparently few of the visitors have been able to resist the temptation to toss something in the well themselves. Coins of Mexico, the United States, and many of the Central American republics came up in great numbers.

Later, a human skull came up the air-lift. Dr. Dàvalos Hurtado examined it and concluded that it was the skull of a girl eighteen or nineteen years old. Her features had been delicate and fine. But, like all Maya children, she had had a board strapped to her head to flatten it in rear and front—to make her more beautiful by Mayan standards.

Many other human remains were dredged up by the air-lift, as well as the skeletons of pumas, deer, jaguars, alligators, and many other animals.

Sometimes the air-lift was less selective. In years gone by, part of the temple on the brink of the abyss had crumbled and fallen into the well, and one day the air-lift sucked up a massive stone from the temple. The tube was clogged and collapsed. The time needed for repairs created a considerable delay.

The work went on for nearly four months. The results were impressive. Thompson had not even begun to exhaust the contents of the sacred well. Among the more than four thousand artifacts that the new expedition had gained for the Government of Mexico were beads of solid gold and jade, a bone knife engraved with Mayan hieroglyphics, a strikingly beautiful jade necklace, several rare dolls and idols, copper medallions inscribed with pictures of the gods, openwork copper rings, and much, much else.

But the sacred well is far from having yielded up all its treasure. Other expeditions in future years will return to this grim place where, hundreds of years ago, solemn Mayan priests hurled fearful victims to destruction while excited multitudes showered the water with their gifts to the gods. One project for the future is the restoration of the temple, but that will be a costly operation, since tons of fallen stone will have to be lifted from the well. Archaeologists hope someday soon to be able to use hydraulic pumps to drain the well completely, so that they will be able to rove the muddy bottom at will, collecting the wealth of material that certainly is still to be found there.

One particular treasure, though, will not be located by the archaeologists of the future. A Maya of today, named Avelino Canul, had served as general foreman for the dredging operations. He seemed so interested in the project that the divers taught him how to use an aqualung. On the very last day of work at the sacred well, Avelino Canul made his first solo dive. He returned to the surface a few moments later, and as he pulled the mouthpiece out, an ear-to-ear grin became visible. He was holding his find proudly aloft: the valuable Rolex watch that diver Fernando Euan had lost three months before!

The Chichén Itzá expedition of 1960 was not the first, though, in which underwater archaeology had been used to recover treasures of the Mayas. Another expedition had done such work several years earlier, in northern Yucatán. Skin divers there explored the sacred well of an important Maya city with the jawbreaking name of Dzibilchaltun.

Dzibilchaltun—pronounced "Dzeeb-eel-chal-*toon*"—gets its name from a Maya word meaning "where there is writing on flat stones." It is one of the largest of the known Maya cities, covering an estimated twenty square miles—more than one-fourth the size of Washington, D.C., and one-third as big as Mexico City.

For years, archaeologists had centered their work in Maya-land around such well known sites as Chichén Itzá and Uxmal, in Yucatan, and Copán, in Honduras. The existence of a major city at Dzibilchaltun was unknown until 1941. In that year, two American archaeologists, E. Wyllys Andrews and the late Dr. George W. Brainerd, visited the site to examine some pottery that had been found nearby. They were amazed to realize that under their feet lay one of the biggest of the Mayan cities, buried by the jungle.

Not only was Dzibilchaltun big; it was old. It had been inhabited long before the time of Christ. Most of the Mayan cities had been built between A.D. 400 and A.D. 1000, but Dzibilchaltun went back much, much further in time. Nor had it been abandoned, the way so many of the jungle cities had; the archaeological evidence showed that the Mayas had lived continuously at Dzibilchaltun for many thousands of years, from perhaps 2000 B.C. until the invasion of the Spaniards in the sixteenth century.

Dzibilchaltun promised to upset many long-standing theories about the Mayas. Originally it had been thought that the early Mayas had lived in the lowland jungles of the south, in Guatemala and Honduras, and had moved north to Yucatán only toward the end of their era. But here was an important Mayan city, unquestionably ancient, far to the north, only seventy-five miles from the relatively young city of Chichén Itzá!

The year 1941 was not a good time for launching major archaeological expeditions. The war effort demanded everyone's devotion. It was not until fifteen years later that Dr. Andrews was able to return to Dzibilchaltun. In 1956, the Mexican government granted Tulane University of New Orleans the right to excavate at Dzibilchaltun for four seasons, and Dr. Andrews headed the expedition.

The archaeologists, after they had made a quick survey of the ruin, were staggered by the sheer size of it. Not much had been visible to the eye, since the jungle had covered many buildings, and recent road-builders had stolen a great deal of the stone and masonry. But as they explored they began to see how much lay under the ground. A ten-square-mile central area was thickly covered with palaces, temples, pyramids, and the stone foundations of vanished thatch huts. Going beyond this main area, the archaeologists found "suburbs" spreading in all directions, with temples and residences galore. The preliminary survey turned up the ruins of more than four hundred buildings in all—and that was recognized as just a small segment of this Mayan metropolis.

It was a staggering city. A giant roadway of limestone, eight feet high and wide enough for four lanes of automobiles, ran down the heart of the city for a mile and a half, linking pyramids and temples of a hitherto unknown type. And a vast palace near this roadway covered more than a dozen acres, bigger than any other Mayan building yet discovered.

Dr. Andrews writes, "To excavate the Palace as a whole was utterly beyond our means; it would take 10 to 15 years of intensive work by hundreds of laborers. But we couldn't help pecking at this buried giant.

"We assigned a crew to dig a single big exploratory trench into what seemed a vast refuse heap behind one wing of the Palace. We were looking for something exceedingly rare in stony, hardpan Yucatan—a deep deposit of undisturbed artifacts capable of giving us a kind of ledger of the long centuries.

"And that is just what we found.

"In a series of cuts only 16 feet wide and 14 feet deep

we recovered nearly 250,000 fragments of pottery—a 'haul' that will require months and years to assess fully."

Dzibilchaltun's archaeological treasures were not all buried in the ground, though. The city had a dozen *cenotes*. The largest of them, in the city's center, was *four times* as deeply filled with water as the huge sacrificial *cenote* at Chichén Itzá. Dr. Andrews sensed with excitement that this great *cenote* almost certainly must hold fabulous archaeological treasure.

In the first season of work at Dzibilchaltun, Dr. Andrews persuaded two vacationing students from the University of Florida, David Conkle and Whitney Robbinet, to don aqualungs and explore the big well. It didn't take them long to find a storehouse of important Mayan artifacts. Pieces of worked flint, carved bone earplugs, jars and pots of great antiquity, and some three thousand pottery fragments were recovered in a few days' time.

A major exploration of the *cenote* was called for.

While one group of archaeologists continued the enormous job of unearthing the buried city, others planned the attack on the *cenote*. The *cenote*—called *Cenote Xlacah*, pronounced "Shla-*cah*" and meaning in Maya "Well of the old town"— was shaped like a tremendous sock, the foot and the toe extending back under a rock ledge. At its widest point, the *cenote* was 100 feet across, and its depth was at least 140 feet. At the 144-foot level, the well twisted off sharply into the rock, continuing for an unknown distance in total darkness.

Yucatán has hundreds of such wells. The whole Yucatán peninsula is overlaid by soft limestone. There are no rivers or streams anywhere in Yucatán, but here and there these huge holes in the limestone have formed and have been filled with fresh water over the centuries. Since these were the only sources of fresh water on the peninsula, the Mayas had to build their cities near important wells.

This is from the account of an adventurous writer, Luis Marden, who entered the well at Dzibilchaltun wearing an aqualung:

"I took a breath of bottled air, slid into the water, and thrust downward toward the yawning black depths. . . . Schools of flat-bodied silvery characin fishes darted round my head as I stared into the darkness. Beneath me the green carpet of tufted water weeds stopped abruptly at the limit of sunlight.

"Under the overhang the darkness seemed almost total at

first. I paused to clear my ears and to turn on the flashlight that hung from my wrist. As my eyes adjusted to the gloom, I could see the vast curve of the roof and back wall receding in a dim semicircle, like an amphitheater seen by moonlight. Under me the rubble-strewn slope dropped at an angle of 50 degrees."

As he continued deeper into the well, Marden, a photographer and writer who has done much notable underwater work, saw carved stones scattered about, Mayan handiwork that might have tumbled into the well a thousand years earlier. Joined by that other skin-diving journalist, Bates Littlehales, he followed down to the "toe" of the sock-shaped well and entered a low, dark tunnel. The depth gauges read 120 feet. "The exhaled air bubbled noisily from our regulators, and when I held my breath, I could hear the expanding silver mushrooms of air glucking and tinkling as they streamed to the rocky vault far above our heads.

"I looked upward. Under the curve of rock the surface opening glowed faintly green, its dim arch of light slashed brutally by the diagonal masses of leaning rock, like monstrous jambs at the gate of some cold and silent hell."

Littlehales made the first discovery. He reached down to haul the broken neck of a jar from the well floor. As it came free, mud roiled up in black clouds, and even by flashlights the two men could see nothing. They signalled each other to return to the surface, since they had been down twenty minutes, the safe limit.

After that first exploration, Marden and Littlehales, accompanied by two Mexican divers, Fernando Euan and Earl Becht, took an anchor to the bottom of the well to create a link with the surface. (It was Euan who was to lose his wristwatch at Chichén Itzá a few years later.) A line attached to the sixteen-pound anchor connected with a diving platform at the surface of the well. The divers could follow this white line up and down while they worked.

A rubble heap began sixty feet down—carved stones of all shapes and sizes. It was as though an entire building had fallen into the well some time in the past. One of the local natives told Marden the legend about the fallen building. It belonged to a Mayan king. One day the king's mother came to him, asking for water. The king, saying he had none to spare, sent her away. "God in His anger," the native explained, "caused the ground to give way under him and his fine house, and they all sank together into the *cenote*. He had plenty of water then."

At the sixty-foot level the divers found basketfuls of broken pots—not very interesting to a layman, perhaps, but of great value archaeologically. Pottery has always been one of the archaeologist's great tools, in every part of the world. Styles of pottery, in the ancient world, tended to remain pretty much the same for decades or even centuries at a time. By comparing the different pottery styles at any given site, archaeologists have been able to work out rough time-tables of age. Though they cannot do more than guess at the exact age of any piece, they can fairly definitely detect which pieces are older than others, and thus work out a scheme of pottery dating that can be employed at other sites in the same area.

The divers picked thousands of pottery fragments, or pot-sherds, out of the rubble heap. To conserve their breathing supply, they would lie head upward on the slope, moving as little as possible. That way they could make their tanks of compressed air last as much as fifty minutes while they filled wire baskets with pottery. The clay was soft and crumbly when it emerged from the water, but it soon baked to hardness under the hot tropical sun.

The divers had to be careful not to disturb any of the large stones of the rubble heap; when they accidentally moved one, small landslides would start, and the divers had to get out of the way. These landslides kicked up clouds of mud that put a temporary stop to any work.

For days, nothing but pottery fragments emerged. Then one day Littlehales found a long bone awl covered with Mayan hieroglyphics—an important piece, even though it is still not possible for archaeologists to read such inscriptions. Several other awls came to light soon afterward. Dr. Andrews thought that they had been accidentally lost by Mayan girls drawing water from the well—but, soon afterward, other objects were discovered that argued a more sinister use for the well. A clay flute, a miniature molded head, noseplugs and other bodily ornaments, then human bones—it began to appear as though sacrifice had been practiced at the well of Dzibilchaltun just as at Chichén Itzá.

It took two weeks to exhaust the rubble heap at sixty feet down. The divers went on to the eighty-foot level. Heads down in the water, they probed armpit-deep in cold ooze and muck for Mayan treasure. Carefully they dug jars from the mud, some of them broken, a few still whole, superb examples of their type. Then Marden found some fragments of coral. Since coral does not grow where sunlight does not reach, these pieces must have been deliberately thrown into the well, perhaps as part of some forgotten religious ritual.

When they were working at sixty feet down, the divers did not have to worry about pressure ailments. They could stay down almost an hour, and make several dives a day, without having to worry about ill effects. As they moved deeper, though, pressure became a force to reckon with. Nitrogen would slowly dissolve into the body, and if a diver came up too fast, stayed down too long, or made too many dives in a single day, the nitrogen would turn to bubbles in the blood, causing paralysis or painful death from "the bends."

Once Marden and Littlehales ventured to the bottom-most point of the well, the 144-foot level. They stayed there only fifteen minutes, and were careful to return to the surface at a speed of twenty-five feet per minute. But this was their third dive of the day, and apparently Marden's system had absorbed more nitrogen than was healthy, even though he had stayed within the safety regulations. Five minutes after surfacing, he felt a twinge of pain in his right arm.

A veteran of seventeen years of diving, Marden knew he must have absorbed too much nitrogen. Losing no time, he strapped a fresh tank of compressed air to his back and descended to the sixty-foot level. He waited there for ten minutes, hoping that most of the nitrogen excess would ebb away. Then he ascended cautiously and slowly. But the pain returned. Down he went again, this time spending twenty minutes at eighty feet. Again, his arm throbbed with pain when he surfaced. He could not go down again; he was blue and shivering with cold. But he was in serious trouble, he knew. He had a case of decompression sickness—the bends.

An engineer rigged an emergency recompression chamber on land, and Marden entered it, along with Littlehales, who felt no pain but was taking no chances. The first chamber could not supply enough pressure, but a second was hastily contrived, and Marden entered it alone. The decompression tables seemed to indicate that he had to spend almost eleven hours at a simulated depth of 165 feet to rid his body of its excess nitrogen. He was sealed into a swelteringly hot oil tank and compressed air was piped in. From time to time his friends would bang on the tank's side, and Marden would feebly bang back to let them know he was still alive, if not exactly comfortable. He was released after six hours and twelve minutes, wilted and soggy. The improvised tank had not been able to simulate a depth of more than one hundred feet. Marden felt better, but he still had the bends. And now Littlehales reported that his back was stiff, and he could not sit up!

The U.S. Consul at nearby Meridá, hearing of the problem, put through a call to Mexico City, and the Ambassador there arranged for a naval plane to pick up both men and fly them to Florida, where the Navy had a recompression chamber. The plane had to fly at only nine thousand feet, since if it went higher, the bubbles in the sick men's blood streams would have expanded, making the situation all the more serious.

They spent forty-four hours and twenty-six minutes in the Navy tank. It was a grueling session—but they emerged cured of the bends, and after a few days' rest they were both able to return to Dzibilchaltun. Their unpleasant experience was a vivid example of the special risks that underwater archaeologists must run.

The final weeks of that year's expedition were fruitful ones. The divers moved down the slope of the well until they reached an unproductive level, then returned to the rubble heap at sixty feet and made a series of interesting finds. A clay jaguar about five inches tall, a nearly intact orangeware dish, a jade bead, a bone with hieroglyphics, a strange wooden mask of which, said Marden, "the puff-cheeked face, with its curious double-topknot hair-dress and wide-open mouth, looked more African than Maya," and many other museum pieces came to light.

The work at Dzibilchaltun is not yet finished. Few archaeological sites are ever totally exhausted, and expeditions return constantly to open up new veins of treasure. Perhaps the well at Dzibilchaltun has given up most of its important contents—but there are many other, smaller, wells at the same city. And the task of excavating the buried parts of the city will keep archaeologists busy for many years to come.

Another site where skin divers have aided archaeologists in casting new light on the Maya civilization is Lake Amatitlan, in Guatemala. Since 1954, skin divers have been recovering Mayan artifacts from this lake, first on an amateur basis, then under careful supervision by professional archaeologists.

Lake Amatitlan was the center of the "highland Maya" civilization, which is much less well known than the "lowland Maya" culture of Yucatán and Southern Mexico. The highland Mayas did not build imposing stone temples and pyramids of the sort that so capture the onlooker's imagination in Yucatan and the lowland jungle cities of Honduras and parts of Guatemala. Their buildings, of sun-baked earth, adobe, and plaster, have crumbled to dust over the centuries, and grass grows over the gentle mounds that once were the palaces of the highland Mayas.

The highland people were also less advanced culturally than the northern Mayas. They did not use the fantastically accurate Maya calendar, the elaborate and fascinating Mayan hieroglyphics, or the impressive Mayan techniques of architecture. For all these reasons, they have been generally ignored by archaeologists until recent years. The bulk of archaeological effort in Central America has been bent toward uncovering the more interesting lowland culture.

A certain amount of digging has been done in the last ten years. But the most interesting highland Maya relics have been found at the bottom of lakes in Guatemala. A nonprofessional archaeologist, diving in April, 1955, in Lake Amatitlan, four thousand feet above sea-level and seventeen miles south of Guatemala's capital, Guatemala City, found an attractive and unbroken pottery vessel. Over the next several years, other skin divers found more than six hundred vessels, incense burners, and stone sculptures.

Word of these finds reached Dr. Stephan F. Borhegyi in 1957. Dr. Borhegyi, a Hungarian-born archaeologist who now lives in the United States, had been conducting an expedition in the highland region that year on behalf of Guatemala's San Carlos University. His interest was aroused by the amateur archaeologists' finds, and he thought at once of making a systematic exploration of the lake along the lines of Jacques-Yves Cousteau's celebrated work at Grand Congloué a few years earlier.

Even before the first skin diver made his find, archaeologists had realized that Lake Amatitlan held Mayan artifacts. Travelers more than a hundred years ago had noted that ancient pottery vessels had turned up by the shore of the lake and in its waters. In 1896, a German archaeologist visiting the lake had seen "curious spiked vessels" found in the lake, and later on other archaeologists, including Dr. Borhegyi, had examined pottery vessels found in the lake by fishermen. But no one suspected just how well stocked the lake was with Mayan antiquities.

Dr. Borhegyi and his group began by mapping the exact

sites of all the underwater discoveries made in the lake since 1955. The lake was divided into an upper and a lower basin, joined by a "bottleneck" channel, narrow and only six feet deep. Nothing of importance had been found in the upper basin, so the archaeologists concentrated on the lower one, where the water varied in depth from 10 to 130 feet.

The archaeologists examined the six hundred-plus objects found by the amateurs. They learned that there were nine separate caches of artifacts—seven of them on the south shore, near bubbling hot springs, and the other two on the north shore.

Luckily for Dr. Borhegyi and his party, the amateurs had kept careful records of their finds, noting down which site each piece came from, and the depth at which it was found. "The specimens," wrote Dr. Borhegyi, "consisted of offering bowls, spiked vessels, and incense burners. They ranged from a few inches to four and one-half feet in height. The incense burners were double-chambered or three-pronged; many bore unusual designs: cacao trees and pods, papaya fruits and flowers, quetzal birds, jaguar heads, spider monkeys, snakes, lizards, bats and even human skulls —motifs hitherto rare or unknown in the highland Maya area. Among the many Maya gods represented were the rain god, Chac or Tlaloc; the jaguar god; the sun god; Eecatl, the wind god (a form of Quetzalcoatl, the feathered serpent); Xipe Totec, a fertility god; and the death god. There were also beautifully executed human heads peering from the jaws of animals and monsters and the beaks of birds."

Once the vessels were classified, Dr. Borhegyi noticed that certain types of pottery came from certain specific sites in the lake. This might mean that each separate site represented a different time period. Each site was near the shore, suggesting that the vessels had been flung into the lake as offerings to the gods.

In order to determine the relative ages of the pottery in the lake, Dr. Borhegyi's group had to re-examine the known archaeological sites on the land surrounding the lake. There were five of these. The oldest one, Site B, had been occupied from roughly 1000 B.C. to A.D. 200. Next oldest was Site C, where fragments of pottery indicated Maya occupancy from A.D. 200 to 600. A much larger site was Site A, on high ground overlooking the west end of the lake, which apparently was occupied from A.D. 200 to about A.D. 1000. Site A consisted of twenty-five different mounds, two of them ball courts where the Mayas had played a game not too different from basketball.

The other two sites, D1 and D2, were on the hillside five hundred feet above Site B. Most of the pottery at these two sites was more than 1200 years old, but some of it was of the type being made when the Spaniards conquered the region in 1524.

The pottery found in the lake could be matched with types of pottery found in each of the five shore sites. This proved that the lake region had been continuously inhabited for over three thousand years. On the evidence of the bowls and incense burners, Dr. Borhegyi was able to work out a history of the region that is probably quite accurate, at least in its general outlines.

He thinks that wandering Mayan tribes settled around Lake Amatitlan some time before 1000 B.C. By that time, they had progressed enough to build houses and make pottery that could survive for thousands of years. Their main occupations were hunting, fishing, and farming. To insure the favor of the gods, whom they thought lived in the lake, they would make gifts of pottery and other objects.

The hot springs and geysers at the south shore of the lake must have encouraged this belief. The sulfurous bubbles and sudden spurts of hot water could easily seem to indicate that supernatural beings dwelled below the surface. And, overlooking the lake, the four-peaked volcano Pacaya smoldered and throbbed, leading the Indians to believe that another god lived in the hills.

Sometime around 200 B.C., the first settlement was abandoned, and the Mayas moved to a different part of the lake, near the hot springs. They built two villages. One of them must have been a religious shrine, since most of the offerings found in the lake were in the style of this village's work.

The volcano probably erupted several times during this period. "Our divers," wrote Dr. Borhegyi, "found bowls in groups of four or five, standing erect and occasionally embedded in lava on the lake floor. This could only mean that to placate the angry gods residing in the volcano these objects had been placed in lava flows near the shore and were thus carried into the lake. Major eruptions, probably accompanied by earthquakes, may have prompted the more extravagant offerings, including human sacrifices."

Skulls and bones seemed to indicate that the Mayas had, from time to time, offered human life to the gods, as they had done so often in the cities of the north. By A.D. 1000, two more settlements had come into being, higher on the hill. A book written in the sixteenth century, the *Account Book of the Town of San Juan Amatitlan*, reveals that the hilltop sites were still inhabited at the time of the Spanish conquest, and even afterward.

Today Lake Amatitlan is involved in a religious ritual that seems to hearken back to Mayan days. A local legend goes that in the days before the Spaniards came, a carved stone idol stood on a cliff on the north shore of the lake. During the seventeenth century, supposedly, a great storm struck the lake and the ancient stone idol sank from sight. The next morning, the pagans who came to the idol's shrine found a wooden statue of the Christ Child in its place.

The wooden statue still exists, and is kept in the church the Spaniards built at Amatitlan. Every May 3, pilgrims come from all over Guatemala. The statuette of the Christ Child is taken from its place in the church and is borne across the waters of Lake Amatitlan to the place where it was found. The pilgrims follow in gaily bedecked boats and canoes, and they throw flowers and fruit into the lake.

A thousand years ago, it was pottery and beads; today, flowers and fruit. In Dr. Borhegyi's words, the "belief that powerful spirits inhabited Lake Amatitlan, and with it the desire to placate these spirits, has survived virtually unchanged over a period of three thousand years. It has managed to withstand or incorporate all foreign religious influences, including Christianity."

The work of the archaeologist is often something like the work of a detective. Both must painstakingly piece together seemingly unrelated clues, until at last they are able to make an informed guess about the particular problem that they have been studying. The pottery vessels found in Lake Amatitlan have helped Dr. Stephan Borhegyi to reconstruct three thousand years of Mayan life in the highland region. Others, using the same careful methods elsewhere, have been able to interpret the story told by potsherds and beads to give us insight into different ancient cultures.

It is certain that the aqualung and the air-lift will play important roles in the future archaeological exploration of Central America. The Maya custom of hurling valuable objects into wells and lakes is now being turned to good account as divers recover these objects by the thousand. The hundreds of *cenotes* and wells in Mexico, Honduras, and Guatemala will undoubtedly yield a rich lode of archaeological information in the years to come.

Chapter 7

A Pirate City in the Sea

Mᴏʀᴇ than 250 years ago, the city of Port Royal, on the beautiful Caribbean island of Jamaica, was considered "the wickedest city in the world." The pirate Henry Morgan had his headquarters here. Striking out from Port Royal, he looted and sacked the rich Spanish cities in the Caribbean region. Other equally bloody pirates liked to frequent the taverns and gambling dens of Port Royal. The town overflowed with pirate gold, stolen from the Spaniards, who had themselves stolen it from the Aztecs and Mayas.

Life was lively in Port Royal. Cutlasses on their hips, pirate captains swaggered down the narrow streets, bellowing raucous songs of triumph. Merchants and innkeepers grew rich as the pirates, gold burning holes in their pockets, spent with a free hand. An account of the town published in 1683 called it "the Storehouse or Treasury of the West-Indies . . . a continual Mart or Fair where all sorts of choice Merchandizes are daily imported. . . ."

The cutthroat Henry Morgan died in 1688, and the town became a little more respectable after that, though it was still no stronghold of virtue. The minister of its church spoke of the town's inhabitants as "a most ungodly, debauched people."

Port Royal was built on a narrow sand bar, a long spit of sand jutting out into the Caribbean. Hundreds of buildings, two to four stories high, covered the sandspit right down to the edge of the sea. Loose gravel had been used to fill in the water and create more land for the expansion of the town.

Winter never comes to the islands of the Caribbean. Twelve months a year, they simmer in hazy sunshine. June 7, 1692, was a typical Jamaican day: hot, sunny, balmy. The perfume of the island's flowers mixed with the salt tang of the sea. The tall inland mountains of the island glimmered in the midday haze. Ships were unloading at Port Royal's docks. The frigate *Swan* rested on her side on land, while her crew lazily scraped at the barnacles fouling her hull. Sailors off duty took care to avoid the tropical sun. Townspeople strolled down the shady streets. It was lunchtime, and most of Port Royal's population was indoors.

Not all, though. One well-to-do gentleman stood at the wharf, and paused to examine his handsome, expensive leather-covered brass watch. He noted that the time was about twenty to noon.

For Port Royal it was the hour of doom.

The entire earth seemed to shudder and go into convulsions. A horrible groaning sound came up from the depths of the earth, a sound that might have been emitted by a giant in agony. From the far-off mountains came a dull booming sound, like thunder, but there was no storm in the offing.

Port Royal trembled in the earthquake's grip.

As though an invisible hand had smitten it, the entire waterfront district was catapulted into the sea. The town's two sturdy forts, Fort Carlisle and Fort James, were engulfed in an instant. Block after block of houses crumpled as the fragile sandspit broke up. Whole streets tumbled into the water. At St. Paul's Church, the bell tower toppled, landing with a jangling crash. The water rose.

Monstrous gullies split the town. As the yawning crevices opened, houses and panicky townspeople were swallowed up. While the earth continued to heave and convulse, a huge wave rolled down over the remainder of the city.

It was as though a divine judgment had been worked against the wicked. In little more than two minutes, two-thirds of Port Royal had been destroyed by the earthquake, and more than two thousand of its people had lost their lives.

The Reverend Emanuel Heath, Rector of St. Paul's, left an eye-witness account of the catastrophe. He wrote, in a letter penned shortly afterwards, that on the fatal day he and John White, Acting Governor of Jamaica, had been about to indulge in some midday wine when the convulsion struck.

"Lord, Sir, what is this?" the Reverend Heath cried out, frightened.

"It is an earthquake," replied Governor White calmly. "Be not afraid, it will soon be over."

Both men survived. As Heath wrote, "In the space of three minutes . . . *Port-Royal*, the fairest town of all the English plantations, the best emporium and mart of this part of the world, exceeding in its riches, plentiful of all good things, was shaken and shattered to pieces, sunk into and covered by, for the greater part by the sea. . . ."

And another account of the times declares, "The earth heaved and swelled like the rolling billows, and in many places the earth crack'd, open'd and shut, with a motion quick and fast . . . in some of these people were swallowed up, in others they were caught by the middle, and pressed to death . . . The whole was attended with . . . the noise of falling mountains at a distance, while the sky . . . was turned dull and reddish, like a glowing oven."

A sudden catastrophe of this kind, in which a town is destroyed in the space of a moment, is a terrible event indeed. But—to be perfectly and cold-bloodedly frank about it—most archaeologists profoundly wish there had been many more such disasters in human history. Our knowledge of the past would be that much more complete.

This seemingly heartless attitude stems from the fact that when a city of the past is left accessible, it suffers through the ages. The marble monuments of Rome were badly harmed over a period of a thousand years by Romans who carted away building-blocks to use in their own homes. This is why Rome's famous Colosseum, for instance, is only a shattered shell. An exposed site means that treasure hunters will come prowling in search of gold, smashing everything that does not interest them. Grazing goats will nibble priceless manuscripts. Children will play catch with precious vases. Dealers in antiquities will carry away whatever they can, for their own profit.

How much more agreeable it is for the archaeologist when everything is destroyed in one moment and hidden from sight, with no chance for further destruction or plunder! The classic example of this is Pompeii, buried under light volcanic ash that did no harm to the buildings and their contents, but that kept looters away for seventeen centuries. Thus the archaeologist Leonard Woolley once wrote, "If the field archaeologist had his will, every ancient capital would have been overwhelmed by the ashes of a conveniently adjacent volcano. It is with a green jealousy that the worker on other sites visits Pompeii and sees the marvellous preservation of its buildings, the houses stand-

ing up to the second floor, the frescoes on the walls, and all
the furniture and household objects still in their places as
the owners left them when they fled from the disaster."

Port Royal was another such archaeologist's dream. A
whole town swept away in a moment—and then buried beneath the waves, where it could come to no further harm
save for watery decay. A complete seventeenth-century
town lay in the waters off Jamaica, sealed by the sea. But
not until recent years did it become possible to recover the
treasures of sunken Port Royal.

The man who rescued Port Royal from the grip of time
was an American explorer, diver, and inventor named Edwin A. Link. In 1956, Link visited Jamaica in his boat,
Sea Diver, and made a preliminary search for the lost pirate
city. He had imagined that the roofs of the buildings of
Port Royal would be visible through the water. But, looking
down, he could see nothing but the muddy bottom, 20
to 40 feet below. Although the Caribbean's water is crystal-
clear, at Port Royal's site mountain streams have carried
tons of mud into the harbor over the centuries, silting it up.

Link designed a new *Sea Diver*, making it the first ship
almost two yards of silt, and came upon the brick walls of
Fort James. But he realized that his equipment was in-
adequate for the job. It was hard to find the buildings of
Port Royal in the silt and mud, and almost impossible to
raise anything from the ruin. He managed to bring up one
of Fort James' canons. Then he left Jamaica to outfit a proper
expedition.

Link designed a new *Sea Diver*, making it the first ship
designed specifically for underwater archaeology. The steel
vessel, ninety-one feet long, was equipped with heavy
booms and electric winches to lift heavy objects from the
sea. Glass plates in the bow afforded a direct view of the
sea bottom. Radar and echo-sounding devices provided the
last word in detection equipment. A special diving compart-
ment, which could be entered both from the deck and the
water, carried a full store of aqualungs, face masks, fins, air
compressors, and all the SCUBA accessories. Aft, *Sea Diver*
carried *Reef Diver*, an eighteen-foot launch propelled by
water jets, that could be used in shallows and reefs.

Before he could begin the salvage operations, Link had
to know what the old city had looked like. Finding
this out proved unexpectedly difficult. There were no maps
of Port Royal in pre-earthquake days to be found. The best
Link could find was a map made in 1827, which claimed

to depict the boundaries of the original city, but which
turned out to be inaccurate. Another map found in the
British Museum was somewhat better so far as providing the
location of the sunken part of the city went, but was still
not good enough. Link saw that he would have to make his
own survey.

For this, he used the launch *Reef Diver*, equipping it
with portable echo-sounding apparatus. A famous navigator,
Captain P. V. H. Weems, joined Link to assist in making the
survey. In June, 1959, they began the job, cruising over the
site of the vanished city and taking depth soundings. Shallower regions could be assumed to represent buildings, deeper ones the spaces between them.

A combination of twentieth-century surveying skill and
seventeenth-century property documents allowed the Link
team to make a fairly accurate chart of the sunken city.
Link knew that the map was not perfect. The city had not
sunk straight down, and in the buffeting of the earthquake
many of the buildings must have been displaced from their
original sites. But the map was good enough to use as a
starter, Link felt.

The diving began.

The first attempt was made on the site of the King's
Warehouse, where valuable merchandise had been stored
in a sprawling group of sheds, not far from Fort James. As
Mrs. Marion Clayton Link writes:

"Excitement ran high that first day when the dredge
went into action, for somehow every one of us expected
to see almost immediate results. There was a rumble deep
in the throat of the air-lift. Then, with a rattling rush of
sound, a powerful jet of debris-filled water burst from its
mouth. It struck the deck of the barge and ran off toward
the edges, leaving muddy patterns of silt and gravel behind.

"By late afternoon a spreading pile of detritus lay on the
barge, dotted here and there with bits of china, pottery,
and broken bottles—all more recent than the earthquake."

Several more days produced the same disappointing results. Nothing came from the air-lift's mouth but mud and
trash. The Links decided that they were probably dredging
an unused area of the 234-foot-long warehouse, or in a part
where perishables like cotton and tobacco and sugar had
been stored. "We might dig forever without striking the section where valuables were kept," Marion Link pointed out.

Back to the map they went. After a lengthy debate they
moved *Sea Diver* to another spot, near the east wall of

Fort James, and lowered the air-lift into the muck once again.

This time there was better luck. Fragments of old wine bottles, pieces of white clay pipes, hunks of coal, bones, bits of flint, bricks, broken dishes, and other seventeenth-century relics began to appear the moment the air-lift started to dig into the silt.

The Links did not let the air-lift do all the work of excavation for them. Too many fragile things might have been damaged on their trip up the metal tube. So, while the divers held the base of the dredge and guided it over the floor of the sea, they would also grope in the mud themselves and endeavor to locate breakable items before the dredge could suck them up.

"Grope" is the right word. The air-lift in operation kicked up a cloud of silt that cut visibility on the bottom down to only a few inches. Even when the big dredge was turned off, the water was so murky that virtually nothing could be seen more than a couple of feet from the diver's face mask. In ten weeks of operations, the water was clear enough for underwater photography on only three days.

The groping divers, working by touch alone, pulled many treasures from the mud—first, a long-handled brass ladle with a perforated bowl, then pewter spoons and plates, and a great many round-bellied rum bottles. The divers reported that they were working near a toppled brick wall on the bottom. There was no doubt that these were relics of the earthquake-shattered city that were being discovered now.

As the work proceeded, the difficulties mounted. Although everyone in the party, including Mrs. Link, was a skilled skin diver, no one had ever had to work in such muddy conditions before. There was always the danger of a sudden cave-in, as the air-lift undermined some already precariously balanced brick wall. The air-lift itself posed a minor problem for the divers. "Many times," wrote Mrs. Link, "the divers' gloves were seized in its greedy maw and deposited on the barge above. We almost expected someday to see the elongated form of the diver himself erupt from the upper end of the pipe." And such natural hazards as barracuda, sharks, and sting rays made life even more interesting for the divers working in murky opaqueness in the ruined city. But no one suffered anything more serious all summer than an injured toe or a squeezed eardrum despite all these menacing complications.

A device which by now is standard operating equipment for any underwater archaeologist proved invaluable to the Port Royal explorers. This was the metal detector, which signals the presence of metal beneath the mud. Link and his divers guided the metal detector over the ocean floor to make many interesting finds. One day, a battered copper pot containing bleached white bones turned up—evidence that someone had been cooking a stew at the very moment the earthquake struck. "You can see the marks of the meat cleaver on the bones," Ed Link commented.

The same spot yielded other kitchen implements—a pewter platter, a grindstone, brass candlesticks, a wooden mortar, the iron grill from a fireplace, and five pots cemented together by the action of the water. It was a kitchen that must have been able to serve a great many people. Consulting their chart, the divers decided that they were either in the cookhouse of Fort James or else in a tavern belonging to one James Littleton—probably the latter.

Examining the material the air-lift had dredged from this kitchen site, an expert from Washington's Smithsonian Institution pointed to a chunk of plaster and remarked that the walls of the building had been wattled—that is, made of twigs, twisted together and tied, and covered over by layers of plaster. The discovery of flat red tiles and blackened bricks served to fill in the rest of the picture. The white plaster building with its red roof must have been one of Port Royal's favorite eating places. Ed Link said, "It would be hard to find another kitchen in the world today with everything just as it was nearly three hundred years ago. On land it would have been destroyed, or at least modernized, long before this. That's the advantage of underwater archaeology."

The U.S. Navy joined the expedition in its second month, contributing half a dozen ace divers. The Navy search team explored the ruins of Fort James looking for weapons. A special heavy-duty hose carried by *Reef Diver* was used to clear away the mud, blasting it away with a jet of water at high pressure, and the divers were able to recover cannon balls of various sizes. The Navy divers also turned up some tumbled walls under the mud east of the warehouses. Here, on the wreckage of a wharf that had once been owned by a citizen of Port Royal named Humphrey Freeman, the divers found one of the onion-shaped rum bottles—unique in that its cork was still in place. A few moments later a second corked bottle came to light, this one also sealed with a twist of brass wire. An experimental shake revealed that the second bottle had something in it.

Like Captain Cousteau, Ed Link could not resist the temptation to sample the elderly brew. And his experience was very much the same. A hypodermic was thrust through the cork to draw off some of the contents of the bottle. Ed Link made a face as he tasted the yellowish fluid. "Horrible," he shuddered. "Tastes like strongly salted vinegar. I guess 1692 must have been a bad vintage year." Cousteau had made the same joke six years before at Grand Congloué.

What amphorae were to Grand Congloué, bottles were to Port Royal. They came up by the hundreds—first, soda bottles of recent date, then nineteenth-century bottles tossed into the water from passing launches and by men on shore, then eighteenth-century rum bottles, dark and round, and finally the distinctive onion-shaped flasks of the pre-earthquake days, often encrusted with coral. One expert remarked that there must be more seventeenth-century bottles at Port Royal than anywhere else in the world. Exposure to the air made the bottles crumble and fall apart, and the Links soon learned to put them in containers of fresh water to preserve them.

One of the most mysterious objects turned up by the divers was a coral-encrusted swivel gun that had been a hundred years out of date at the time of the earthquake. It was the kind of gun that had been in use in the fifteenth century in Spain. Had someone in Port Royal been a collector of antique guns? The Spaniards had settled a few colonies on Jamaica's north shore in the sixteenth century; perhaps this was a gun they had brought with them. Ed Link offered another guess, which can never be proved or disproved but which excites the imagination. "It could have come from one of Columbus' ships when he had to strand them in St. Ann's Bay on the north shore," he said. "When the Admiral and his men were finally rescued, they must have had to leave everything behind except their most essential belongings."

The gun that might have belonged to Columbus was one of the most enigmatic of the expedition's discoveries. But by far the most important find was a much smaller object— so small that the divers groping in the mud had not even noticed it. It turned up in the debris spewed up by the air-lift, and was spotted by a sharp-eyed Navy diver as it lay in the muck.

It was a gleaming brass watch, crusted over by its centuries in the sea. Its delicate brass gears and other fine parts were still uncorroded and clean. When the coral that had grown over the face of the watch was removed, it was possible to make out the numerals of the hours, in silver. The hands of the watch had long since disintegrated. But an X-Ray of the coral that had covered the dial showed an imprint of the hands, one pointing at the eight, one at the twelve.

Ed Link studied the watch and the X-Ray for a moment. "It stopped at seventeen minutes of twelve," he said finally. "Just time enough for the water to have reached the works after the earthquake struck."

But suppose the watch had been lost long after the earthquake? The Links had no way of telling. Engraved on the inner side of the case was the name of the maker, Paul Blondel. Some checking revealed that Paul Blondel was a Dutch watchmaker who had stopped making watches in 1686. Later that season, Ed Link took the watch to the Science Museum in London, where one of the world's greatest collections of old watches is kept. After conferring with museum experts, Link cabled back this news:

WATCH AUTHENTICATED BY SCIENCE MUSEUM TO BE BY PAUL BLONDEL AMSTERDAM 1686 WHO WAS HUGUENOT REFUGEE FROM CHALONS STOP TIME SHOWN BY WATCH 17 MINUTES TO NOON IS REGARDED AS AUTHENTIC TIME OF EARTHQUAKE

The elegant brass watch, once covered by a leather case, was the finest of the *Sea Diver's* finds. But the horde of spoons and pots and pipes gave invaluable information about the life of the doomed city on its last day.

The Links had to call their expedition to a halt after ten weeks. It was hurricane time in Jamaica, now, and further work would be too risky. They had achieved a great deal in that short time. They had compiled an accurate map of the sunken city and had salvaged hundreds of important artifacts. For all that, though, they had only made a beginning. "It would take years of steady effort," Ed Link said, "to make a thorough search. . . . Think of the houses, the taverns, the shops of all kinds, the King's storehouse, the warehouses, and the ships which sank at the docks. Why, it's probably the richest known archaeological site of its period in the world today."

The lure of other places called the Links away. But the archaeological treasure of Port Royal still remains, safe beneath the warm Caribbean, and before long, another team will dive down to continue the exploration. The pioneering work of Ed and Marion Link and their associates has opened the way. Sooner or later, Ed Link noted, "somebody will go back there and be rewarded with such an array of both artifacts and riches as to make our effort seem trivial."

Doubtless the Links' finds will be overshadowed by the objects that emerge from the Port Royal site in the future. But the word "trivial" is one that can never be applied to the Links' efforts, except by an overly modest man like Ed Link himself. He showed the way. The future explorers of sunken Port Royal will always be indebted to him.

Chapter 8

The Warship Vasa Returns
from the Sea

A<small>UGUST</small> 10, 1628, was a bright, hot Sunday in Sweden—a good day for a gala event like the launching of a great galleon. And the new warship about to join Sweden's navy was truly magnificent, a sight to inspire fear in the hearts of the foe and pride and awe in the breast of every Swede. The *Vasa* was her name, called after the family of Sweden's warrior-king, Gustavus Adolphus.

The *Vasa* was the new flagship of Sweden's Home Squadron. The Thirty Years' War raged in Europe then, that complex, bewildering struggle that left half the continent devastated when it finally sputtered to its finish in 1648. In 1628, Sweden was not yet deeply involved in the war, but the hero-king Gustav was already planning the brilliant campaigns that would make him the savior of Protestant Europe until his death in battle a few years later. He needed warships to protect the Baltic. The *Vasa* was a giant, 1400 tons, 165 feet long at the deckline, 40 feet in the beam. "Building small ships is only a waste of young trees," the king had declared.

The *Vasa* bore sixty-four guns—forty-eight massive bronze cannons jutting through double rows of gunports along her sides, and sixteen smaller guns in the open on the top deck. The hatch of each gun port was decorated with the head of a roaring lion, painted a brilliant gold, its mouth fiery red. The gun decks, too, were painted red, to hide the sight of the blood that would flow on them when the ship engaged in battle. The bowsprit thrust thirty feet outward, and below it, on the prow, a gilded lion, poised to spring, gleamed impressively in the figurehead position.

The brilliant sunlight of that August day in 1628 must have set off the *Vasa's* gaudy golden and red trim to splendid advantage. Crowds had gathered on the quay to watch the mighty ship get its first taste of the sea. For months, the ship had been moored at the dockside, taking on provisions for a year's voyage. She carried two thousand barrels of food-stuffs and beer, gunpowder, supplies of all sorts. Now it was time for the maiden voyage. The *Vasa* had a crew of 133 sailors. As passengers, three hundred soldiers and their wives and children were aboard.

The *Vasa's* captain, Severin Hansson, was worried about the design of his ship. It was long and thin—too long, he thought, too thin to support the enormous weight of the 180-foot-high mast and the rest of the vessel's ponderous super-structure. A few weeks before the launching, Captain Hansson had conducted a little test of his own while the *Vasa* rested in her mooring. He had sent a couple of dozen sailors aboard and ordered them to run across the deck from port to starboard. As they did so, their weight made the ship heel more than a foot. As they ran back, she swung two feet back toward portside. Crossing the deck a third time, the sailors caused the *Vasa* to list three feet. Captain Hansson called off the test at that point, fearful that the sailors would capsize the ship altogether.

Sweden's Grand Admiral, Klas Fleming, had watched that test. But he had made no comment. King Gustav was eager to see his proud new ship asail. It had been three years in the building, and the king had waited impatiently for its completion. No one dared tell him now that a launching might be risky.

So the ceremony proceeded on schedule. At 3 P.M. on August 10, the troubled Captain Hansson gave the order to cast off. A gentle southwesterly breeze fluttered across the harbor at Stockholm. The *Vasa*, carrying many dignitaries who expected to be put ashore the next day at a nearby is-land, was towed to a point along the south shore of the harbor. Only some of her complement of sails were broken out.

The moment the breeze caught the sails, the *Vasa* veered and heeled wildly to port. The ship's ordnance officer, Erik Jonsson, who was as worried about the ship as his captain, sped belowdecks to make sure the heavy cannon were se-curely lashed down. If they broke free and rolled to one side of the ship, the *Vasa* would capsize.

The ship righted itself quickly enough, as the passengers moved around to restore the balance. More sail was let out, and as the breeze caught the canvas the stately vessel moved serenely out of the harbor. Captain Hansson ordered the small cannon on the main deck to be fired. A battery on shore boomed a congratulatory reply, and the dockside watchers cheered.

A moment later, a strong gust of wind bellied out the sails, and again the ship listed far to port. A second time, Erik Jonsson hurried below.

"She's going to capsize!" a sailor bellowed.

"Quick!" Jonsson ordered. "Unlash the cannons! Move them to windward!"

The sweating sailors untethered the big guns and strained to push them up the slanting deck and counterweight the heeling ship. But it was too late. Water began to pour through the open gunports. The cannons broke loose from the sailors' grasp and rolled back, crushing them against the hull. Still the ship heeled to port, until half her bottom had rolled into view. As the water continued to flood the hull, the *Vasa* abruptly went down. The whole episode had lasted but a moment. The cheers of the watchers on shore turned abruptly to gasps of horror and astonishment.

The *Vasa* had gone no more than 4500 feet on her maiden voyage. Now she rested on the bottom in 110 feet of water. She had nearly righted herself as she sank, and her giant masts jutted above the waves, bearing Sweden's imperial flag on high in cruel mockery.

Boats quickly put out from shore to rescue the sailors and passengers. Most of those aboard were saved, but at least fifty went down with the ship.

The victims were hardly in their graves when the first attempt at salvage was made. The Council of the Realm named Ian Bulmer, an English engineer, to raise the ship. He tried, looping hawsers around the wreck's masts and using horses in a vain attempt to drag the ship from the water. He succeeded in pulling the ship into a completely upright position, but had no luck in getting it from the water. Other would-be salvagers, Swedish, French, English, Dutch, and German, had an equal lack of success. Most of them ended up losing their anchors, cables, and grappling irons, which wound themselves around the wreck.

Meanwhile, a court of inquiry was trying to place the blame for the fiasco. Captain Hansson had been jailed after the sinking. But at the inquiry he mentioned the tests he had run the month before, with sailors moving back and forth over the wobbling deck. "Had they run more times," one of the ship's officers corroborated, "the ship would have capsized at the dock." And Erik Jonsson, who had been badly battered by the water and the sliding cannons, but who had survived all the same, testified that "if she had not been under sail she would even so have capsized . . . as she was heavier topsides than below."

The court of inquiry then turned up two uncomfortable facts: that Grand Admiral Fleming had witnessed the stability tests in July, and that King Gustav himself had approved the plans for the ship. It became awkward to press the inquiry any further. No one in the court had any wish to embarrass people in high places. Captain Hansson and his officers went free, and the matter was quietly dropped. Today, some experts still blame faulty design for the sinking, while others believe that the tragedy could have been avoided if the cannons had been placed more intelligently.

Be that as it may, the ship had gone down. In 1663, a Swedish group made a new attempt at salvage. They developed a diving bell in which a diver could stand, breathing air at the top of the chamber while using the grappling hooks. Working in fifteen-minute stints in bitterly cold water, the divers, at depths of nearly one hundred feet, ripped away the timbers of the main deck and attached grapnels to the cannons. In April, 1664, the first cannons came to the surface, and before they finished, the salvagers had recovered fifty-three of the Vasa's sixty-four guns, a valuable prize indeed.

After that, the world forgot about the Vasa. It seems hard to believe that so spectacular a catastrophe could slip from everyone's memory. Yet it did. Two and a half centuries passed, and the recollection of the warship's sinking vanished from the minds of men. The great hulk lay in Stockholm's harbor, unknown and unmarked. Now and then a ship would foul her anchors on the wreck, and over the years more than thirty anchors were lost in that way. But no one seemed to know or to care what obstacle on the harbor bottom was causing all the trouble.

The story was rediscovered in the twentieth century. A Swedish historian, Nils Ahnlund, was examining old archives in search of information on an entirely different matter. He stumbled across the minutes of the court of inquiry that had investigated the Vasa's sinking, and then found an account of the sensational diving-bell salvage of 1663–64. It was a startling discovery: that a fully outfitted seventeenth-century ship lay buried somewhere in Stockholm harbor!

Among those whose imaginations were captured by Professor Ahnlund's revelation was a boy named Anders

Franzén. His father, a Stockholm physician, told him th
story. Young Franzén would spend his summer vacations, a
the family cottage near Stockholm, searching the shallo
water for bits of wreckage, and often he would find frag
ments of old sailing ships, waterlogged but recognizable

In 1939, Franzén and his family spent the summe
cruising off Sweden's west coast, and there he found woo
that had been eaten by teredos, or shipworms. Teredos ar
not really worms at all, but a kind of clam. They burrov
their way into submerged wood and actually eat the wood
In the United States alone, teredos do more than $50,000,
000 of damage to boats and docks each year. Naturally
they are the bane of the underwater archaeologist, destroy
ing much priceless material.

Young Franzén wondered why the wood he had found
near Stockholm showed no sign of teredo damage, while i
the waters to the west teredos seemed to flourish and ea
everything they could reach. Checking, he learned tha
teredos can only live in water with a salt content of 0.9
or more. The Baltic's salinity is only 0.7 on the average, and
in some places much less.

It was an encouraging discovery. If the waters around
Stockholm were free of teredos—why, then, perhaps the
Vasa, still intact, could be found and lifted!

He kept the idea in the back of his mind for many
years. It would be an expensive job, and he certainly did
not have the funds for it in 1939. Besides, no one ever
knew the exact location of the Vasa.

Franzén became a petroleum engineer. He studied nava
history as his hobby, though, and when SCUBA became
available he learned how to skin dive. Compiling a list of
more than fifty ships known to have been wrecked off the
east coast of Sweden, he narrowed the number to about a
dozen, and began looking for them. His first project was the
salvage of the Riksäpplet, a big warship that had sunk in
Dalarö Harbor, near Stockholm, in 1676. With the co-opera-
tion of Stockholm's National Maritime Museum, Franzén explored the Riksäpplet, which lay in only fifty feet of water.
But ice and waves had smashed the ship to fragments, and
local people had carried off many of her timbers.

Next he turned to the Vasa, which lay in deeper, calmer
waters. Professor Nils Ahnlund told him, "Find Vasa, and
you will have the greatest treasure of all."

But where did the ship lie?

Franzén wrote, "By 1954 . . . I had amassed a huge

mount of research data and was ready for an all-out attack. Using borrowed and hired motorboats, I began a systematic sweep of the bottom with grapnels and wire drags. Crews aboard harbor craft became accustomed to the sight of a lonely figure engaged in a strange kind of fishing. They laughed when I brought up old bedsteads, tires, stoves, Christmas trees, and the like."

A contour map of the bottom of the harbor had been drawn, using echo-sounding gear, for the benefit of engineers planning a bridge across the harbor. Franzén noted that a large hump was located a hundred yards south of a navy drydock on the harbor island of Beckholmen. Franzén asked the engineers about the hump.

"Oh, it must be just debris left when they blasted out the drydock," they told him.

Franzén turned now to the historical archives. It had occurred to him that King Gustav had been out of the country, fighting in Poland, when the *Vasa* sank. Surely someone must have sent a letter to the monarch telling him about the disaster. Sure enough, he uncovered a copy of the report of the Council of the Realm, dated August 12, 1628, two days after the sinking, bearing the unwelcome tidings to the king. The report said, "And when she came out into the bay by Tegelviken there came more wind into her sails . . came to Beckholmen sudden, where she entirely fell on her side and sank in 18 fathoms of water."

Beckholmen!

And that suspicious hump near the drydock—was it really only debris of blasting?

Franzén had designed an instrument to help him in his quest—a "core sampler." This was a six-pound steel cylinder, bomb-shaped, and containing a sharp hollow punch in its nose. When he dropped it into the water, the punch would cut a slice out of anything it landed on.

Usually the sampler had brought up nothing but mud. Sometimes it came up with a core of wood, but not ancient wood. The *Vasa's* hull was made of oak, and oak turns black after a century or more of submersion.

Franzén hurried in a motorboat to the site of the hump on the harbor bottom. It was a fine August day in 1956, almost 328 years to the day since the sinking of the *Vasa*. He threw his sampler overboard. Down it went, more than one hundred feet down, and struck. Heart pounding, he reeled it up.

Its punch contained a plug of black, close-grained oak.

There could be no doubt now. He had found a ship several centuries old. He had found the *Vasa*.

To make sure he had not simply sampled a single sunken plank, Franzén dropped his sampler over a broad area. Each time it came up with a plug of oak. He went immediately to the Royal Swedish Navy. The Navy's Divers' School was located at the drydock, only three hundred feet away. It was an easy matter for him to persuade the Navy to shift its training operations to the site of the *Vasa*.

The first Navy diver to go down was Chief Diver Per Edvin Fälting, a veteran of more than ten thousand hours of diving. Fälting sent up a gloomy report by telephone to the anxious Franzén, waiting on the diving vessel 110 feet above him. "I'm standing in porridge up to my chest. Can't see a thing."

He was about to come up when an accidental twitch on his lifeline from above sent him dropping twenty feet into deeper mud. Reaching out for support, he touched something solid. "It feels like a wall of wood," he telephoned. "It's a big ship, all right! Now I'm climbing the wall . . . here are some square openings . . . must be gunports."

Climbing higher on the hull, Fälting found the upper row of gunports as well. This erased the last doubt. No other known wreck in the vicinity had had a double tier of gunports. This had to be the *Vasa*.

The news electrified Sweden. In a moment the entire country was catapulted three and a half centuries back in time, to the great era when Sweden was a major imperial power in the world and all Europe trembled before the armies of Gustavus Adolphus.

Fälting found that the wreck stood upright, embedded in hard clay to the waterline. The masts, though broken, still thrust surfaceward. In the loose mud covering the upper part of the ship were the irons and chains of the seventeenth-century salvagers. An underwater television camera, lowered into the mud-clouded water, relayed a blurred but unmistakable image of the mighty ship for those waiting above.

A bold idea took hold in Sweden: why not try to raise the ship in one piece and restore her to her former glory— not as a warship, of course, but as a titanic museum piece?

It would be a formidably expensive job. But no one in Sweden seemed upset by the cost. Sweden's popular king, Gustavus VI, a remote descendant of that old Gustav, was himself a trained archaeologist, and his enthusiasm became infectious.

The Neptun Salvage Company of Stockholm offered to contribute its services free of charge to lift the ship— $500,000 worth of work performed simply to restore this relic of Sweden's past. The Royal Swedish Navy assigned its divers to the operation as a training exercise. Contributions of labor or cash came from all over the country, until the $2,000,000 cost of the project was easily covered.

There were to be two main stages in the salvage operation. First, the wreck would be lifted from her depth of 110 feet and shifted to more accessible waters where she would rest at a convenient 50 feet. There, she would be repaired and strengthened, made watertight so that she could be lifted to the surface.

Captain Axel Hedberg of the Neptun Salvage Company was in charge of the first stage of the project. His plan involved blasting six big tunnels into the bottom next to the *Vasa's* hull, completely under the ship's keel, and up the other side. Then steel cable could be passed through these tunnels and fastened to salvage pontoons on the surface. When the pontoons were pumped out, they would rise, pulling the cables taut and lifting the ship.

It was, in Anders Franzén's words, "one of the most complicated and perilous" jobs in diving history. The ship's hull was full of rock ballast. If the timbers of the hull gave way, tons of rock would shower down on the divers as they worked. More than two thousand man-hours of work were carried out, though, without a serious injury. The divers— in helmet-suits, not aqualungs, because of the extreme cold of the water—carved the six tunnels with powerful water jets that sliced through the muck at the bottom. Suction hoses pumped the debris to the surface, where archaeologists sorted through it for material of value. Hundreds of elaborate carved figures, once attached to the hull, had fallen off over the years, and now came to the surface via the suction hoses as the divers worked. Smaller items, such as pewter mugs, clay pipes, a sundial, and coins, came to light during this stage of the work.

Some of the divers were superstitious and believed that the wreck was haunted. *Den Gamle*—"The Old One"—was the ghost of a sailor who still lived in the wreck. The Old One was supposedly annoyed at being disturbed. To soothe him, the divers would throw copper coins into the water each day before starting work. But still they feared The Old One. One diver, using the water jet to make a tunnel under the keel, suddenly felt his diving helmet, normally almost weightless under water, grow tremendously heavy. He could not understand what was crushing down on him this way.

"The Old One has me," he chattered, panicky, into the helmet telephone.

On the diving barge, Chief Diver Fälting heard him and snapped, "Stop it. Don't panic. If The Old One has you, be calm and go like a man." Then, calming the diver enough to get a description from him of what was happening, Fälting said, "You are caught in a pocket of your own air." The diver was relieved to get such a simple explanation for the occurrence. He crawled out of the tunnel and returned safely to the surface, perhaps still suspecting that it had all been some prank of The Old One.

The Old One stayed his hand, and by August, 1959, after two summers of work, the tunnels were complete and the cables were in place, attached to the salvage pontoons *Oden* and *Frigg*. It was an uneasy moment. Would the old ship, heavily burdened by mud, resist the pull of the cables and come to the surface, or would it collapse into shattered timbers at the first pull?

The signal was given. Pumps began to spew water from the pontoons. As they emptied, they rose higher from the water, pulling the slack cables taut. A diver went down to inspect the situation.

"*Vasa* has lifted eighteen inches, all in one piece," he reported. "All well."

She was clear of the bottom. With infinite care the salvagers moved the ship toward nearby Kastellholmen (Castle Island). Her keel was four feet above the bottom as she moved up an easy slope. Gradually, she was drawn into shallower water. It took eighteen lifts, over a period of twenty-seven days, before she came to rest in fifty-foot water where she could be reached easily for restoration.

The first stage—and the riskiest—was successfully completed. Now came the less dangerous, but infinitely more difficult, task of restoring the *Vasa*. A committee of archaeologists supervised the work. First, divers went down to clear away the debris—the anchors that had been fouled on the wreck, the abandoned salvage equipment of past centuries, and the mud and skeletons of the crew. A dozen well-preserved skeletons were recovered, along with muskets, earthenware, wooden dishes, leather boots, a cockaded felt hat, and even casks of butter. Over a two-year span, the divers boarded up the gunports, made repairs to the damaged stern of the ship, and caulked all leaks in the hull. Their work made the ship reasonably watertight again.

The archaeologists, meanwhile, were sorting out and classifying the contents of the hull and were taking steps to preserve the perishable wooden statuary by soaking the carvings in arsenic and carbon wax.

The second stage of the salvage operation was finished in the spring of 1961. It was time, now, to lift the *Vasa* to the surface.

Frogmen fastened four inflatable rubber pontoons to the *Vasa's* keel. These would give the ship buoyancy. Steel cables, nine inches in diameter, were slipped under her hull and attached to jacks on the pontoons. Then the ship was jacked upward out of the water. She rose fifty feet and broke the surface for the first time in 333 years one day in April, 1961. Franzén and Fälting climbed into a small boat and rowed out to inspect the ship as she cleared the water, while on the shore, watchers cheered and a Navy band played a fanfare. Solemnly, Franzén clambered out onto the main deck, the first living man to stand on its timbers in three centuries. Then grinning, the unsuperstitious Franzén took a copper coin from his pocket and hurled it into the water-filled hold of the ship. "An offering to The Old One," he explained.

It took a month of cautious coaxing to bring the *Vasa* to shore. Listing slightly to port, she was towed into the drydock at Beckholmen and mounted on a concrete platform. A sprinkler system went into operation to keep the ship wet, for if she were allowed to dry out at this point the timbers would quickly rot.

At the present time, Swedish archaeologists are working to preserve the ship by spraying the wood with polyethylene glycol. This waxy substance will force the moisture from the timbers and keep them from deteriorating. The archaeologists are also still pumping the mud from the ship, shoveling it through wire sieves so that nothing of value will be lost. Later, divers will explore the wreck site in an attempt to recover the elaborate wood carvings which dropped into the mud when the ship sank, as well as the treasure chest of gold that is believed to have been on board. In several years' time, the *Vasa* will be restored completely to her appearance of 1628. The again-proud vessel, gleaming in fresh gold and red paint, will be placed on display in a concrete-and-glass structure near Beckholmen—a museum ship showing exactly what a seventeenth century war vessel was like. However, the job of restoration may take as many as ten more years.

Among the items salvaged from the hull was a bottle of rum of 17th-century vintage. In the summer of 1962, when former President Eisenhower visited Sweden and toured the *Vasa*, he was offered a taste of this rum by Anders Franzén. But Ike smilingly declined the offer, and settled for a mere sniff. "It's amazing," he commented.

During his inspection of the ship's carvings and fittings, General Eisenhower noticed that the wooden lion of the ship's figurehead had no tongue. He provoked laughter by remarking, "Maybe it would be better if some of us also did not have a tongue."

The Swedish public seems mostly interested in the ship's treasure and in the skeletons. Archaeologist Anders Franzén finds this an amusing attitude. "Everyone wants to see the treasure, and no one realizes you can see it already. This is the treasure—the ship itself. People are excited by skeletons and gold coins, the two things which historians and scientists care least about. We have graveyards full of 17th-century skeletons and many collections crammed with 17th-century coins.

"But now we have a complete 17th-century community, frozen in place by disaster and preserved by the sea. It will tell us so many things. We don't know how they built ships in the early 1600's, because there was no science of naval architecture and no one left drawings to tell us. We don't know how the sailors lived aboard ship in those days. We don't know what kind of navigation instruments they used. We don't even know what the Swedish flag looked like in 1628."

As the mud is cleared from the wreck of the *Vasa*, some of these blanks in our knowledge will at last be filled. The giant warship was a miniature city in itself. And now, like Pompeii in Italy or Port Royal in Jamaica, it has been found and uncovered, and soon we will know just how it looked on the day disaster overtook it.

Chapter 9

Cities Beneath the Waves

THE scope of underwater archaeology, as outlined in the previous chapters, is certainly an impressive and wide-ranging one. But underwater archaeologists are both excited and a little overwhelmed by the truth about their profession: that it has only just begun.

An incredible amount of work still remains. Whole kingdoms must be reclaimed from the sea. On land, the job of the archaeologist today is basically to follow up the great work of his predecessors, to amplify and clarify and provide more detail, more illumination. The basic work has been done. Troy and Nineveh and Babylon can only be found once. Those who follow after can add greatly to the work of the earlier archaeologists, but they cannot make many new, spectacular finds.

It is not the same in underwater archaeology. Each year sees new expeditions that uncover fertile new fields for exploration. And other areas, half-legendary, still await a visit from the men in the aqualungs.

For instance, the sunken city of Ys, on the northern coast of Brittany, in France. Ys is a city of myth, of legend, of mystery. Even its very name has a magical sound, conjuring up ancient sorceries.

The legend says that Ys was a rich and powerful city, thousands of years ago. It was the westernmost outpost of civilization, in that far-off, time-misted era. Situated on an inlet, the city was protected from the sea by a dike that held the waters back. The ships that made Ys wealthy could enter the harbor through a lock in this dike.

The king of Ys, so the legend runs, was King Gradlon, a wise and honest ruler. His daughter, the beautiful Dahut, was wicked and sinful. One day, she stole the golden key to the dike, and went to visit her lover. Time sped in her lover's arms, and in the meanwhile the tide came in. The lock could not be closed without the missing key. The sea rushed through the open gates, drowning the city of Ys with all its riches, drowning King Gradlon and the fair but evil Dahut.

Why did Dahut steal the key? This, the legend does not tell us. That part of the story has been lost with time, through thousands of retellings over hundreds of years. But was there an Ys? Is the story just a pretty myth, or does it have a kernel of truth, just as Homer's *Iliad* tells the fanciful story of a real war between real cities?

Yes. There *was* an Ys. Perhaps it had no King Gradlon, no Princess Dahut. But the city existed and was drowned by the sea, along with many others along the Breton coast. Fishermen of the village of Cancale will show visitors the ruins of walls on the bottom of the sea near their town. "That is Ys," the fishermen will say, and they will tell the story of Princess Dahut. But the fisherman are wrong. The walls near Cancale are the remains of the citadel of Gardoine, which resisted the army of Charlemagne during a siege, only to be swept away by a flood. Gardoine was flooded in the ninth century. Ys died long before.

Roman settlers had inhabited the coast of Brittany in the early centuries of the Christian era. A Roman map of A.D. 400 showed Ys, perched at the edge of the sea on the Bay of Douarnenez. It is possible to sail out into the bay on a clear day and see the Roman road itself, running straight out from land and into the water, submerged by some long-ago flood. When the tide is low, the remains of walls and perhaps foundations can be seen. Ys may have been drowned by the flood that is known to have ravaged Brittany in A.D. 395, or by the even more dreadful flood of 441.

Divers have had no luck exploring the city of Ys. The waters off Brittany are deep and cold, the weather uncertain. A French expedition explored the Bay of Douarnenez after the Second World War, and found nothing—not even the blocks of masonry that were supposed to be there. The city of Ys remains unfound, along with many other less magical cities of Roman Brittany. Work for some future underwater archaeologist, here. Half a dozen lost cities, weedchoked and inhabited by coiling octopi, may wait in the cold waters for their rediscoverer.

Another elusive sunken city is Helike, which has been called "the underwater Pompeii." Helike was a city of Greece, ancient enough to have been mentioned in the *Iliad*.

Like Pompeii, Helike was suddenly destroyed—not by a volcanic eruption, though, but by an earthquake and a flood.

The double catastrophe struck in 369 B.C. First came the earthquake, then the flood. Pausanias, a Greek historian of the second century after Christ, described the tragedy this way:

"First the ground was shaken to the depths by an earthquake, then suddenly it opened up and everything which was built upon it collapsed and plunged into the depths, no trace remaining thereafter. Thus perished Helike.

"It is said that this earthquake was followed by another disaster, caused this time by the season of the year: the overflowing of the sea, which inundated the town and the surrounding countryside. The sacred wood of Poseidon was so submerged that one could hardly see the tops of the trees therein. The wrath of God struck the unhappy town through two elements, first shaking it to the ground and then engulfing it with all its inhabitants."

For hundreds of years thereafter, the ruins of Helike and its neighboring town, Bura, were visible in the sea, off the Gulf of Corinth. Many classical writers mentioned having seen the temples and columns of Helike beneath the clear water. But two rivers flow down from the hills nearby, carrying silt. Over the centuries, this deposit of silt completely buried Helike.

An archaeological expedition visited the site in 1950. Four French divers went down to look for the ruins of Helike. But mud covered everything. A German destroyer had been sunk off the site in 1941, and even that, in only nine years, had been nearly buried in silt. How many more feet of silt must cover a town that was drowned twenty-three centuries ago!

The 1950 expedition had to abandon the idea of excavating Helike. At least twenty feet of hard-packed mud covered the city, and in 1950 no equipment existed for removing such a massive layer of slime, especially at depths of up to 125 feet. Today, suction-pump devices such as the Link Air-Lift could cut through Helike's shroud of mud with relative ease. But the formidable task of excavating the city would take many months and cost, perhaps, a million dollars. With other, more inviting sites waiting to be explored, Helike has been left for a future date.

"If you seek Helike and Bura, the lost towns of Achaea, then look beneath the sea," wrote the Roman poet Ovid two thousand years ago. Helike and Bura still wait beneath the sea for their exhumation. When the effort to recover them is finally made, the yield will be a rich one. The French archaeologist R. Demangel, writing about Helike, leaves the tempting knowledge that "a whole town dating from the fourth century B.C. with its ramparts, the furniture of its houses, the statues in its sanctuaries and the skeletons of its inhabitants" lies in wait for some energetic digger of the future.

Another project for the future is the recovery of the Pharos, the great lighthouse of Egypt that once ranked as one of the Seven Wonders of the ancient world. The Pharos, at Alexandria on the Mediterranean, was erected about 279 B.C. by a Greek architect, Sostratus. It served both as a lighthouse and as a public monument. More than five hundred feet high, it was crowned by a colossal statue of the god of the sea, Poseidon.

The Pharos remained in working order for almost a thousand years. Then earthquakes toppled it into the Mediterranean. All that remained of the mighty structure, which had awed Caesar, Mark Antony, and countless other visitors to Egypt, was its stump, some fragments of red granite. In 1480, Egypt's Sultan, Kait Bey, built a castle and fortress on the lighthouse's site. The remnants of the Pharos were embedded in the walls of Kait Bey's castle.

The shattered ruins of the lighthouse are still lying on the floor of the sea in Alexandria's harbor. No one knows where. Skin divers have explored the harbor thoroughly, and have found many items of archaeological interest—Roman coins, granite columns, coffins of marble.

Early in 1962, a young Egyptian skin diver slipped into the water to spear some fish. He was only a few yards off shore, at a depth of twenty-four feet, when he spied fragments of a very large statue—one piece alone was twenty feet long. Near it, he came upon a smaller statue, a column, and a sphinx.

Dr. Henry Riad, curator of the Greco-Roman Museum at Alexandria, suggested that the huge statue might be that of Poseidon, which once had topped the Pharos. If so, it could be that the ruins of the entire lighthouse lay buried nearby!

The United Arab Republic Navy sent divers down, and they confirmed the original diver's report of statuary of colossal size. But the water was too rough, and too muddy to permit photographing of the ruins. Commented Dr. Riad, "In Egypt we have long experiences with antiquities found in the desert. But working under a rolling sea is new and strange to us."

Further work in charting the area had to be postponed for six months, until the fall, when the sea would be at its calmest. Once the charting is complete, recovery work can begin—and perhaps the Pharos will be hauled from the sea after seven hundred years of submersion.

Not far from Alexandria geographically, but a million miles away politically, is the site of the ancient city of Caesarea. Once, both Alexandria and Caesarea were part of the Roman Empire, but today Alexandria lies in Egypt, Caesarea in Israel. The two nations are enemies, and so the two cities lie in hostile worlds.

Caesarea was built by Herod, King of the Jews, in 10 B.C. He was not the Herod we know from the Bible, but the father of the king who delivered Christ to the crucifiers. Before Herod built his city there, an ancient Phoenician town called Iol stood upon the site. Herod tore Iol down and built a port of entry for Palestine. The Jewish historian Josephus, who saw Caesarea nineteen hundred years ago, wrote, "(Herod) erected many edifices with great diligence all over it, and these of white stone. He adorned it with the most sumptuous palaces and large edifices for containing the people. . . . The city was of a fine structure; nay, the very subterranean vaults and cellars had no less of architecture bestowed on them than had the buildings above ground. . . . Herod also built a theatre of stone; and an amphitheatre capable of holding a vast number of men. . . ."

At its peak of glory, Caesarea was a city of 100,000. It was a major Mediterranean port, bustling with life, swarming with merchants of a dozen nationalities. Pontius Pilate had his official residence at Caesarea. The Romans ruled there for six centuries. In 639, the Arabs conquered the city, and turned it into an opulent Moslem port. Five hundred years later, the Crusaders descended on Caesarea, drove out the Arabs, and ruined much of the city. A century and a half later, the Arabs reconquered it. Instead of inhabiting the city themselves, the Arabs chose to destroy it completely. They wrecked the fort the Crusaders had built, and smashed one of the two ancient aqueducts that had brought water to Caesarea. A flood was turned loose. Caesarea became a swamp. Mud and dank marsh covered its splendid palaces. The unimportant town of Cherchel sprang up in the ruins.

Traces of Roman Caesarea remained visible—a jetty in the harbor, a tower here, a column there. But drifting sand covered most of the Roman city, and the nibbling action of the waves caused much of the harbor to crumble into the sea. Archaeologists had done some work to recover ancient Caesarea, including some aqualung exploration in the early 1950's. But the most important expedition to Caesarea was conducted in 1960—61 by Edwin A. Link, the man who had previously discovered Port Royal.

Link used his ship, *Sea Diver*, which is so admirably equipped for underwater archaeology. His air-lift dredged tons of sand away from the Roman ruins bringing up amphorae, coffins, coins, bits of jewelry. Diggers on land found an Arab treasure vault of the eleventh century, containing gold jewelry and pendants of glass, agate, and carnelian. The dredge came up with such unusual items as ivory hairpins, a unique lamp, bronze nails, and a dime-sized medal that showed a view of the port as it had looked in Herod's time. Another important discovery was a handsome Roman mosaic floor, which Link uncovered by blasting away the sand that covered it with his special high-pressure hose.

Much still remains at Caesarea, both on land and in the sea, but Ed Link's expedition made an important beginning and was a major contribution to the always booming field of Holy Land archaeology. Future air-lift explorations will undoubtedly do much to reveal Herod's city on the Mediterranean.

Other sites for underwater archaeology abound in all parts of the world. Five thousand years of shipwrecks lie at the bottom of the Mediterranean, and only a few of the hundreds or even thousands of wrecks have been located thus far. In Egypt, many important ancient sites will be flooded when the new Aswan Dam is completed, and an entire new vista for underwater archaeology will open up there. Dams built in the United States have flooded several sites of American Indian life, and skin divers will be needed to explore those. Off the coast of Syria, off North Africa, off France—wherever men of ancient times built close to the sea, there are ruins beneath the waves. The aqualung, the air-lift, the underwater metal detector, and other technological advances will make the task of the archaeologist that much easier as the work progresses. The number of still-untouched sites numbs the mind. The underwater archaeologist need never fear that he will, like Alexander the Great, run out of new worlds to conquer.

But one site remains not only untouched but undiscovered. It may not even exist, except in the realms of fantasy. No one who has ever strapped on an aqualung has failed to wonder, probably, whether he will be the one to discover Atlantis—the fabled lost continent.

Atlantis is pure myth, so far as we know. Plato first spoke of it, in his two dialogues, *Timaios* and *Kritias*. He told the story of the mighty empire of Atlantis, on an island of immense size somewhere to the west of Greece. The Atlanteans, Plato related, had conquered many of the lands around their own huge island, but their sway was cut short when an earthquake and flood caused Atlantis to sink beneath the sea. Plato put the time of Atlantis' sinking at about 9000 years before his own day, or some 11,500 years ago. He said that he had heard the story from a descendant of the early Athenian statesman Solon, who had learned of Atlantis from some priests in Egypt.

Plato was a man of poetic bent, and quite probably he was deliberately creating a myth for the sake of illustrating his philosophic ideas. But perhaps not.

We do not know. But we do know that the concept of Atlantis has been seized upon and embroidered down through the centuries. Atlantis has become the empire of frauds and quacks who have falsely claimed to have discovered it. Some "experts" have claimed that the Mayas of Central America were refugees from sinking Atlantis; other, even more fanciful theories have been put forth.

Tracing the history of the Atlantis concept is a tedious task. One expert on Atlantis and its mythology has compiled a list of more than 150 authors who have written explanations of Plato's Atlantis passages. The bibliography of Atlantis is almost endless.

The fact that in every century since Plato's time men have speculated about Atlantis, dreamed of finding Atlantis, and even gone in search of it, indicates the hold that this legendary continent has on the imagination of mankind. Myth it may be, but a fascinating myth it is. Many peoples have legends of a great flood, and of a continent sinking beneath the waves. The persistence of these myths in widely separated parts of the world points to some actual catastrophe in the remote past, perhaps the sinking of a group of volcanic islands, that could have been translated in the retelling into the disappearance of an entire continent.

We have no evidence. Atlantis may be nothing but a gorgeous fairy tale. If there is a shred of reality to the story, though, it could well be that our century—the century of underwater archaeology—will see its discovery. In a hundred sunken corners of the globe, men today are prowling for lost ships, lost villages, lost cities. Who is to say that one of them may not come upon the most fabulous prize of all underwater archaeology—a lost continent?

We must not be carried away by dreams of fantasy. There is plenty of down-to-earth diving and digging for the underwater archaeologists to do. They need not go chasing off after fabled Atlantis while Helike and Ys still remain unexcavated, while most of Port Royal lies under Caribbean mud, while Mayan wells still hold secrets of the past. But perhaps—by accident, some day—a probing diver will stumble across the jutting columns or broken walls of storied Atlantis, and the world will gasp anew, as it did when Troy and Nineveh were reclaimed from time's grasp.

In the world of fiction, of course, Atlantis has been found many times. Never more vividly has it been described, though, than in that century-old classic of underwater exploration, Jules Verne's *20,000 Leagues Under the Sea*. It may seem odd to end a book of fact with a quotation from a novel of fantastic fiction. But this is a case where fiction not only rivals the excitement of reality, but almost surpasses it. Remember that at the time Jules Verne wrote, underwater archaeology was a dream, aqualungs a fantasy, and most of the great discoveries of land archaeology yet to be made. The far-seeing Verne managed to set down in fictional guise an unforgettable glimpse of the thrill that may await some flesh and blood archaeologist of a few decades hence. I include the scene here because it seems to me a stirring fictional re-creation of the mystery and romance of underwater archaeology.

That night about eleven o'clock, I received a most unexpected visit from Captain Nemo. He asked me very graciously if I felt fatigued from my watch of the preceding night. I answered in the negative.

"Then, M. Aronnax, I propose a curious excursion."

"Propose, Captain?"

"You have hitherto only visited the submarine depths by daylight, under the brightness of the sun. Would it suit you to see them in the darkness of the night?"

"Most willingly."

"I must warn you the way will be tiring. We shall have far

to walk, and must climb a mountain. The roads are not well kept."

"What you say, Captain, only heightens my curiosity; I am ready to follow you."

"Come then, sir, we will put on our diving-dresses."

Arrived at the robing-room, I saw that neither of my companions nor any of the ship's crew were to follow us on this excursion. Captain Nemo had not even proposed my taking with me either Ned or Conseil.

In a few moments we had put on our diving-dresses; they placed on our backs the reservoirs, abundantly filled with air, but no electric lamps were prepared. I called the captain's attention to the fact.

"They will be useless," he replied.

I thought I had not heard aright, but I could not repeat my observation, for the captain's head had already disappeared in its metal case. I finished harnessing myself. I felt them put an iron-pointed stick into my hand, and some minutes later, after going through the usual form, we set foot on the bottom of the Atlantic, at a depth of 150 fathoms. Midnight was near. The waters were profoundly dark, but Captain Nemo pointed out in the distance a reddish spot, a sort of large light shining brilliantly, about two miles from the Nautilus. What this fire might be, what could feed it, why and how it lit up the liquid mass, I could not say. In any case, it did light our way vaguely, it is true, but I soon accustomed myself to the peculiar apparatus. . . .

As we advanced, I heard a kind of pattering above my head. The noise redoubling, sometimes producing a continual shower, I soon understood the cause. It was rain falling violently, and crisping the surface of the waves. Instinctively the thought flashed across my mind that I should be wet through! By the water! In the midst of the water! I could not help laughing at the odd idea. But indeed, in the thick diving-dress, the liquid element is no longer felt, and one only seems to be in an atmosphere somewhat denser than the terrestrial atmosphere. Nothing more.

After half an hour's walk the soil became stony. Medusae, microscopic crustacea, and pennatules lit it slightly with their phosphorescent gleam. I caught a glimpse of pieces of stone covered with millions of zoophytes and masses of sea-weed. My feet often slipped upon this viscous carpet of sea-weed, and without my iron-tipped stick I should have fallen more than once. In turning round, I could still see the whitish lantern of the Nautilus beginning to pale in the distance.

But the rosy light which guided us increased and lit up the horizon. The presence of this fire under water puzzled me in the highest degree. Was it some electric effulgence? Was I going towards a natural phenomenon as yet unknown to the savants of the earth? Or even (for this thought crossed my

brain) had the hand of man aught to do with this conflagra-
tion? Had he fanned this flame? Was I to meet in these depths
companions and friends of Captain Nemo whom he was going
to visit, and who, like him, led this strange existence! Should
I find down there a whole colony of exiles, who, weary of the
miseries of this earth, had sought and found independence in
the deep ocean? All these foolish and unreasonable ideas pur-
sued me. And in this condition of mind, overexcited by the
succession of wonders continually passing before my eyes, I
should not have been surprised to meet at the bottom of the
sea one of those submarine towns of which Captain Nemo
dreamed.

Our road grew lighter and lighter. The white glimmer came
in rays from the summit of a mountain about 800 feet high.
But what I saw was simply a reflection, developed by the clear-
ness of the waters. The source of this inexplicable light was a
fire on the opposite side of the mountain.

In the midst of this stony maze, furrowing the bottom of
the Atlantic, Captain Nemo advanced without hesitation. He
knew this dreary road. Doubtless he had often traveled over it,
and could not lose himself. I followed him with unshaken confidence. He seemed to me like a genie of the sea; and, as he
walked before me, I could not help admiring his stature which
was outlined in black on the luminous horizon.

It was one in the morning when we arrived at the first
slopes of the mountain; but to gain access to them we must
venture through the difficult paths of a vast copse.

Yes; a copse of dead trees, without leaves, without sap, trees
petrified by the action of the water, and here and there over-
topped by gigantic pines. It was like a coal pit, still standing,
holding by the roots to the broken soil, and whose branches,
like fine black paper cuttings, showed distinctly on the watery
ceiling. Picture to yourself a forest in the Harz, hanging on to
the sides of the mountain, but a forest swallowed up. The
paths were encumbered with sea-weed and fucus, between
which grovelled a whole world of crustacea. I went along,
climbing the rocks, striding over extended trunks, breaking the
sea bind-weed which hung from one tree to the other; and
frightening the fishes, which flew from branch to branch. Press-
ing onward, I felt no fatigue. I followed my guide, who was
never tired. What a spectacle! How can I express it? How paint
the aspect of those woods and rocks in this medium—their
under parts dark and wild, the upper colored with red tints,
by that light which the reflecting powers of the waters
doubled? We climbed rocks, which fell directly after with gigantic bounds, and the low growling of an avalanche. To right
and left ran long dark galleries, where sight was lost. Here
opened vast glades which the hand of man seemed to have
worked; and I sometimes asked myself if some inhabitant of
these submarine regions would not suddenly appear to me.

But Captain Nemo was still mounting. I could not stay behind. I followed boldly. My stick gave me good help. A false step would have been dangerous on the narrow passes sloping down to the sides of the gulfs; but I walked with firm step, without any feeling of giddiness. Now I jumped a crevice the depth of which would have made me hesitate had it been among the glaciers on the land; now I ventured on the unsteady trunk of a tree, thrown across from one abyss to the other, without looking under my feet, having only eyes to admire the wild sites of this region.

There, monumental rocks, leaning on their regularly cut bases, seemed to defy all laws of equilibrium. From between their stony knees, trees sprang, like a jet under heavy pressure, and upheld others which upheld them. Natural towers, large scarps, cut perpendicularly, like a "curtain," inclined at an angle which the laws of gravitation could never have tolerated in terrestrial regions.

Two hours after quitting the Nautilus, we had crossed the line of trees, and a hundred feet above our heads rose the top of the mountain, which cast a shadow on the brilliant irradiation of the opposite slope. Some petrified shrubs ran fantastically here and there. Fishes got up under our feet like birds in the long grass. The massive rocks were rent with impenetrable fractures, deep grottos, and unfathomable holes, at the bottom of which formidable creatures might be heard moving. My blood curdled when I saw enormous antennae blocking my road, or some frightful claw closing with a noise in the shadow of some cavity. Millions of luminous spots shown brightly in the midst of the darkness. They were the eyes of giant crustacea crouched in their holes; giant lobsters setting themselves up like halberdiers, and moving their claws with the clicking sound of pincers; titanic crabs, pointed like a gun on its carriage; and frightful-looking poulps, interweaving their tentacles like a living nest of serpents.

We had now arrived on the first platform, where other surprises awaited me. Before us lay some picturesque ruins, which betrayed the hand of man, and not that of the Creator. There were vast heaps of stone, amongst which might be traced the vague and shadowy forms of castles and temples, clothed with a world of blossoming zoophytes, and over which, instead of ivy, sea-weed and fucus threw a thick vegetable mantle. But what was this portion of the globe which had been swallowed by cataclysms? Who had placed those rocks and stones like cromlechs of prehistoric times? Where was I? Whither had Captain Nemo's fancy hurried me?

I would fain have asked him; not being able to, I stopped him—I seized his arm. But shaking his head, and pointing to the highest point of the mountain, he seemed to say—

"Come, come along; come higher!"

I followed, and in a few minutes I had climbed to the top,

which for a circle of ten yards commanded the whole mass of rock.

I looked down the side we had just climbed. The mountain did not rise more than seven or eight hundred feet above the level of the plain; but on the opposite side it commanded from twice that height the depths of this part of the Atlantic. My eyes ranged far over a large space lit by a violent fulguration. In fact, the mountain was a volcano.

At fifty feet above the peak, in the midst of a rain of stones and scoriae, a large crater was vomiting forth torrents of lava which fell in a cascade of fire into the bosom of the liquid mass. Thus situated, this volcano lit the lower plain like an immense torch, even to the extreme limits of the horizon. I said that the submarine crater threw up lava, but no flames. Flames require the oxygen of the air to feed upon, and can not be developed under water; but streams of lava, having in themselves the principles of their incandescence, can attain a white heat, fight vigorously against the liquid element, and turn it to vapor by contact.

Rapid currents bearing all these gases in diffusion, and torrents of lava, slid to the bottom of the mountain like an eruption of Vesuvius on another Terra del Greco.

There, indeed, under my eyes, ruined, destroyed, lay a town—its roofs open to the sky, its temples fallen, its arches dislocated, its columns lying on the ground, from which one could still recognize the massive character of Tuscan architecture. Farther on, some remains of a giant aqueduct; here the high base of an Acropolis, with the floating outline of a Parthenon; there traces of a quay, as if an ancient port had formerly abutted on the borders of the ocean, and disappeared with its merchant vessels and its war-galleys. Farther on again, long lines of sunken walls and broad deserted streets—a perfect Pompeii escaped beneath the waters. Such was the sight that Captain Nemo brought before my eyes.

Where was I? Where was I? I must know at any cost. I tried to speak, but Captain Nemo stopped me by a gesture, and picking up a piece of chalk stone, advanced to a rock of black basalt, and traced the one word,

ATLANTIS

What a light shot thought my mind: Atlantis, the ancient Meropis of Theopompus, the Atlantis of Plato, that continent denied by Origen, Jamblichus, D'Anville, Malte-Brun, and Humboldt, who placed its disappearance amongst the legendary tales admitted by Posidonius, Pliny, Ammianus Marcellinus, Tertullian, Engel, Buffon and D'Avezac. I had it there now before my eyes, bearing upon it the unexceptionable testimony of its catastrophe. The region thus engulfed was beyond Europe, Asia, and Lybia, beyond the columns of Hercules, where those powerful people, the Atlantides, lived, against whom the first wars of ancient Greece were waged.

Thus, led by the strangest destiny, I was treading under foot the mountains of this continent, touching with my hand those ruins a thousand generations old, and contemporary with the geological epochs. I was walking on the very spot where the contemporaries of the first man had walked.

Whilst I was trying to fix in my mind every detail of this grand landscape, Captain Nemo remained motionless, as if petrified in mute ecstasy, leaning on a mossy stone. Was he dreaming of those generations long since disappeared? Was he asking them the secret of human destiny? Was it here this strange man came to steep himself in historical recollections, and live again this ancient life—he who wanted no modern one? What would I not have given to know his thoughts, to share them, to understand them! We remained for an hour at this place, contemplating the vast plain under the brightness of the lava, which was sometimes wonderfully intense. Rapid tremblings ran along the mountain caused by internal bubblings, deep noises distinctly transmitted through the liquid medium were echoed with majestic grandeur. At this moment the moon appeared through the mass of waters, and threw her pale rays on the buried continent. It was but a gleam, but what an indescribable effect! The captain rose, cast one last look on the immense plain, and then bade me follow him.

We descended the mountain rapidly, and the mineral forest once passed, I saw the lantern of the Nautilus shining like a star. The captain walked straight to it, and we got on board as the first rays of light whitened the surface of the ocean.

For Further Reading

No BOOK of less than two hundred pages could do more than begin to tell the exciting story of underwater archaeology. I hope that this book will serve as an interesting enough introduction to send the reader on to further researches of his own, to understand this fascinating subject in greater detail. For the benefit of such readers, here is a list of further reading material.

CHAPTER 1

For information on the field of archaeology in general, especially the highlights of its early phases, see my earlier book, *Lost Cities and Vanished Civilizations*, which deals specifically with the archaeological discoveries at Pompeii, Troy, Crete, Babylon, Chichén Itzá, and Angkor. (Chilton, 1962.)

For older readers, the standard popular work is C. W. Ceram's *Gods, Graves, and Scholars*—a lengthy, detailed, but unflaggingly exciting survey of archaeology in many parts of the world. (Knopf, 1951.)

The best single book on skin diving, its techniques, problems, and accomplishments, is *Mask and Flippers*, by Lloyd Bridges and Bill Barada. This book briefly but comprehensively covers the entire story of diving apparatus in readable and accurate fashion. (Chilton, 1960.)

A valuable and wonderfully interesting book on the overall subject of undersea exploration, from the earliest days to the present, is *Man Under the Sea*, by James Dugan. Several interesting chapters on underwater archaeology are to be found in this volume. (Harper, 1956.)

CHAPTER 2

The story of the finds at Antikythera and Mahdia is told in detail in *4,000 Years Under the Sea*, by Philippe Diolé. Diolé, himself an underwater archaeologist, provides first-hand accounts of many of his own archaeological adventures in the Mediterranean. (Messner, 1954.)

Man and the Underwater World, by Pierre de Latil and Jean Rivoire, is a good overall survey of underwater exploration, and touches on Antikythera and Mahdia. (Putnam, 1956.)

Derek J. de Solla Price tells the story of the Antikythera computing machine in his article, "An Ancient Greek Computer," *Scientific American,* June, 1959.

The Silent World, by Jacques-Yves Cousteau with Frederic Dumas, provides an account of Cousteau's adventures under the sea, including his work at Mahdia. Few more engrossing scientific adventure stories have ever been written. (Harper, 1953. Cardinal paperback edition, 1955.)

The Living Sea, by Cousteau with James Dugan, continues the story of Captain Cousteau's adventures. (Harper, 1963.)

CHAPTER 3

Norbert Casteret's own book, *Ten Years Under the Earth,* contains the best account of his exploration of the cave at Montespan. Casteret also told his story in an article published in the *National Geographic Magazine,* August, 1924, called, "Discovering the Oldest Statues in the World." The article is worth looking for, because it includes many photographs of the cave and its contents.

CHAPTER 4

The story of the work off Grand Congloué was told by Captain Cousteau in his article for the *National Geographic Magazine* of January, 1954, "Fish Men Discover a 2,200-year-old Greek Ship." This article contains many superb underwater color photographs taken by Captain Cousteau and his divers. Cousteau and Dugan's *The Living Sea* gives a more detailed account of the Grand Congloué operations.

Philippe Diolé's *4,000 Years Under the Sea,* while it makes only slight mention of Cousteau's Grand Congloué expedition, discusses ancient Greek and Roman shipping in great detail and even provides an appendix showing the different types of amphorae. Some of the material in this book may be too specialized for the casual reader.

Scientific American for November, 1954, contains an article by Lionel Casson entitled, "Trade in the Ancient World," which is a clear and concise account of Greek and Roman shipping routes, with a map and several interesting photographs.

CHAPTER 5

Readers who want to find out more about the civilization of the Mayas, which is also discussed in Chapter 5 of my *Lost Cities and Vanished Civilizations,* can turn with benefit to a pair of inexpensive paperback books: *World of the Maya,* by Victor W.

von Hagen (Mentor Books, 1960), and *Maya,* by Charles Gallen-kamp. (Pyramid Books, 1962.)

The story of Edward Herbert Thompson's exploration of the sacred well at Chichén Itzá is told in T. A. Willard's book, *The City of the Sacred Well,* published by Century in 1926, and by E. H. Thompson himself in his *People of the Serpent,* published by Houghton Mifflin in 1932. The objects which Thompson found in the well are on display at the Peabody Museum of Archaeology and Ethnology at Cambridge, Massachusetts, on the campus of Harvard University.

CHAPTER 6

John Lloyd Stephens' account of his adventures in Maya territory, *Incidents of Travel in Central America, Chiapas, and Yucatán,* was first published in 1841. Old editions of this lengthy but fascinating book can be found in second-hand bookstores, but the complete book was reprinted in a modern edition in 1960 by the University of Oklahoma Press and is still in print.

The story of the 1960 Mexican expedition to Chichén Itzá is told in two articles in the October, 1961 *National Geographic Magazine:* "Return to the Sacred Cenote," by Eusebio Dàvalos Hurtado, and "Treasure Hunt in the Deep Past," by Bates Little-hales.

The *National Geographic* also contains a pair of good accounts of the Dzibilchaltun expedition, in the January, 1959 issue: "Dzibilchaltun, Lost City of the Mayas," by E. Wyllys Andrews, and "Up from the Well of Time," by Luis Marden.

An excellent account of the Lake Amatitlan operations and the highland Maya civilization in general can be found in Stephan F. Borhegyi's article in the March, 1959 *Scientific American,* entitled, "Underwater Archaeology in the Maya Highlands."

CHAPTER 7

Marion Clayton Link's account of the excavation at Port Royal is to be found in the *National Geographic Magazine* for February, 1960, under the title, "Exploring the Drowned City of Port Royal." The well-illustrated article is particularly useful because it contains an elaborate reconstruction of Port Royal as it looked on the day of the earthquake.

Mrs. Link's book, *Sea Diver,* published by Holt, Rinehart & Winston in 1959, describes the Link family's earlier adventures in underwater archaeology and salvage.

CHAPTER 8

Two good magazine articles provide a detailed story of the *Vasa's* raising. The *Saturday Evening Post* for October 21,

1961, includes an article by Don Schanche called "The Strange Affair of the Vasa" that covers the subject very well.

Archaeologist Anders Franzén's own account of the project of salvaging the *Vasa* was published in the *National Geographic Magazine* for January, 1962, under the title, "Ghost from the Depths: the Warship *Vasa*."

The complete *Vasa* story is told in book form in *Vasa: The King's Ship*, by Commander Bengt Ohrelius. (Chilton, 1963.)

More information on teredos can be found in Charles E. Lane's article, "The Teredo," *Scientific American*, February, 1961.

CHAPTER 9

Helike, Ys, and many other sunken cities, both real and mythical, are discussed briefly in *Vanished Cities*, by Hermann and Georg Schreiber. (Knopf, 1957.) Diolé's *4,000 Years Under the Sea* also mentions these cities.

Diolé also cites the early work done by himself and others at Caesarea. A preliminary report on the Links' 1960–61 Caesarea expedition was published in *Life*, May 5, 1961, as "Sea Search into History at Caesarea," by Kenneth MacLeish. The article is illustrated by many handsome color photographs.

High Dam Over Nubia, by Leslie Greener, is the best single source of information on underwater archaeology in Egypt, particularly in the light of the flood to be caused by the new Aswan Dam. (Viking, 1962.)

The definitive book on the Atlantis myth is *Lost Continents: The Atlantis Theme in History, Science, and Literature*, by L. Sprague de Camp. (Gnome Press, 1954.) Because it was issued by a small publishing house, this classic book may be hard to find, but it well repays the search for anyone interested in Atlantis in particular or archaeology in general. It is scholarly in scope but well-written and marvelously entertaining.

The extract from Jules Verne's *20,000 Leagues Under the Sea* came from Chapter IX, "A Vanished Continent."

Index

Plato, 4, 14, 28, 115, 120
Pliny, 120
Poland, 103
Polyethylene glycol, use of, 107
Pompeii, 19, 90, 110, 111, 120, 122
Port Royal, 4, 72, 88–97, 116, 124
Poseidon, 111, 112
Posidonius, 120
Pottery, 49, 50, 78, 80, 84, 85
Prehistoric statues, 29–39
Preservation of discoveries, 49, 50, 106–108
Pressure, underwater, 5, 6, 12, 25
Price, Derek J. De Solla, 15, 16, 123
Prieur, Yves, 7
Provence, 44
Pump, underwater (see Air lift)
Pyramid, at Chichén Itzá, 59, 60
Pyrenees, 30, 37

Quetzalcoatl, 84

Rebreathing devices for divers, 6–9, 37
Recompression chamber, 47, 48, 81, 82
Reef Diver, 91, 92, 94
Regulators, demand, 8
Reinach, Salomon, 3, 19
Relación de las Cosas de Yucatán, 58, 59
Riad, Henry, 112
Riksäpplet, 102
Rivoire, Jean, 123
Robbinet, Whitney, 78
Rolex wristwatch, 74, 76, 79
Roman Empire, 113
Romans, 3, 4, 26
  in Britain, 38
  in Caesarea, 113, 114
  in France, 110
  in Greece, 14, 20, 40, 44
  shipping of, 123
Rome, 13, 16, 20, 41, 53, 90
Romero, Pablo Bush, 71
Rouquarol, Benoist, 8

Sacrificial wells (see Wells)
St. Ann's Bay, 95
St. Paul's Church, Port Royal, 89
Salazar, Ponciano, 73
Samos, 27
San Carlos University, 83
Saturday Evening Post, The, 124

Schanche, Don, 125
Schreiber, Hermann and Georg, 125
Scientific American, 123–125
SCUBA divers (see Aqualungs)
Sculpture, at Chichén Itzá, 67
Scylla, 41
Sea Diver (book), 124
Sea Diver (ship), 91, 92, 114
Servanti, Pierre, 47, 48
Sestius, Marcus, 40–54
Shipping, Greek and Roman, 40–42, 123
Shipworms, damage from, 49, 102, 125
Shipwrecks, 3
  at Antikythera, 12–16, 19, 20, 26, 27
  at Cape Artemision, 23–26
  at Grand Congloué, 41–52, 83, 95, 123
  at Kythera, 27
  at Mahdia, 16–23, 122, 123
  in Mediterranean, 114
  in Sweden, 98–108, 124
Shore areas, submerged, 4
Sicily, 41
Silent World, The, 9, 123
Skin diving (see Aqualungs)
Smithsonian Institution, 94
Socrates, 14
Sodom, 4
Solon, 115
Somersetshire, 38
Sostratus, 112
Soulitzes, 25
Spain, 3, 55
Spanish conquistadors, 56, 73, 76, 85, 86, 88
Speleology, 29–39
Sponge divers, 11–28
Stadiatis, Elias, 11, 12
Stais, Valerios, 14
Stamires, George, 15
Statues, in Alexandria harbor, 112
  at Antikythera, 12–16
  at Cape Artemision, 24
  at Kythera, 26, 27
  prehistoric, 29–39
Stephens, John Lloyd, 57, 58, 124
Stevenson, Robert Louis, 21
Stockholm harbor, 98–108
Stockholm National Maritime Museum, 102
Sulla, 14, 20
Swan, 89

If you enjoyed this book, you'll want to read these other exciting Bantam Pathfinder Editions.

Other Bantam titles you are certain to enjoy